*Psychoanalytic
Sociology*

PSYCHOANALYTIC SOCIOLOGY / *An Essay on the Interpretation of Historical Data and the Phenomena of Collective Behavior*

FRED WEINSTEIN *and*
GERALD M. PLATT

The Johns Hopkins University Press
Baltimore and London

The Johns Hopkins University Press, Baltimore, Maryland 21218
The Johns Hopkins University Press Ltd., London

Library of Congress Catalog Card Number 72-12860
ISBN 0-8018-1462-6 (clothbound edition)
ISBN 0-8018-1463-4 (paperback edition)
Manufactured in the United States of America

Originally published, 1973
Johns Hopkins Paperbacks edition, 1973

Library of Congress Cataloging in Publication Data will
be found on the last printed page of this book.

Contents

For Our Parents

Preface

The present work is directed toward the development of a theory of social change based on the integration of various psychoanalytic hypotheses and assumptions with normative sociology. The purpose of this work is to establish the usefulness of certain aspects of psychoanalytic theory for historical and sociological endeavor. Because it is necessary, in terms of these disciplines, to stress interaction between and among individuals and groups—which is not a central concern of classic psychoanalysis— and because it is necessary also to stress such factors as change as a function of temporal processes and the flexibility of personality, it is our task to abstract from psychoanalysis those themes which are particularly pertinent to these dimensions of analysis. This often leads away from themes which Freud himself considered to be of paramount importance. However, the fact is that many emphases and concerns of the contemporary ego psychology tend to do the same, and are for that reason much more consistent with the requirements of historical and sociological endeavor.

We have addressed ourselves to the problem of change in an earlier work, *The Wish To Be Free*. In that work we explained social change in terms of a nurturance-subordination scheme in which passive relationships to authority are acted upon without critical reflection (i.e., mandates are not available for conscious examination and repudiation) as long as nurturant and protective obligations are fulfilled on the part of authority. We stated that, when the morality binding the situation is violated, for whatever reason, the conditions are established for radical demands against the environment. However, there are instances of change other than those characterized by nurturance-subordination. We are therefore stating now that *any* internalized network of standards and expectations creates a situation of psychic stability, and that the disruption or loss of this network can lead to radical activity.

Further, we now consider that violation of the morality as such (i.e., superego transgression) is not a sufficient basis for radical reactions.

Rather, violation must affect all psychic-structural levels (id, ego, super-ego, identity), not only in terms of the morality, but also in terms of internalized standards for ego activity and in terms of the ego's standards for drive activity.

In our earlier work we assumed also that ambivalence was the fundamental situation underlying the differentiation process. But this means that the basic motivation for change is in its sources instinctual. We have taken the position here that id processes are structured to a significant degree by cultural and social influences so that codified expression of new standards and expectations derives from the external world via processes of identification and internalization. That is, the content expressed existed initially in the external world, and the basic problem is not one of universal and immutable drives finding an appropriate moment to achieve expression.

It should be understood at the outset that our focus here is on the theoretical issues involved. It is clear to us, of course, that observation, not theory as such, is the basis of any discipline. It is also clear that a lot has been written by now on psychosocial studies and on psychohistory. What we are still faced with, however, is a mass of unassimilated data pertaining to social change which needs as much to be organized and brought under control as it needs to be added to. Theory facilitates the selection and organization of data, it points to new ways of looking at data, and so forth. On the other hand, we are far from satisfied with what has been offered so far as psychohistory and as theoretical legitimation for this type of work. There is still in much of what is done (in spite of Erikson's contribution) a fundamental contradiction between the need to analyze *interaction* and *external reality* and the emphasis on drive theory which directs attention away from the influences of these factors. Clarification of the theoretical issues is therefore justified.

We are indebted to a number of people for their support, suggestions, and advice. We would like to mention in particular Talcott Parsons, whose pioneering efforts in the integration of psychoanalytic and sociological thought paved the way for our own work; Clifford Geertz, who pointed out the pitfalls in certain lines of thought and helped thereby to formulate some of our views; Professor Platt's graduate students who participated in his seminar in History and Sociology at the University of Massachusetts, Amherst, for their criticism of earlier versions of these chapters; and a committee of concerned scholars which met under the auspices of the American Academy of Arts and Sciences to discuss the development of psychohistory in 1970–71. The committee read and commented on an earlier version of the third chapter of this book. A number of scholars were involved in the work of this committee, which was chaired by William Langer and Bruce Mazlish. We would like to thank the chairmen and all those members of the committee who shared with us their insight and criticisms.

Professor Weinstein would also like to thank the Research Foundation of the State University of New York for providing the summer grant which was used to get this work underway; and the Institute for Advanced Study, Princeton, N.J., the institute's director, Carl Kaysen, the Carnegie Corporation, and the Russell Sage Foundation for providing the time and resources needed to put this work together in final form.

Psychoanalytic
Sociology

I. The Problem in Outline

The issues raised by the use of psychoanalytic propositions in historical and sociological work are not easily resolved. It seems quite evident now that both historians and sociologists intend to make systematic use of psychoanalytic theory in their work; indeed, it is no longer a question of employing various suggestions in a random way but of mastering another highly complex discipline.[1] Still, the theory is not readily accommodated either to history or to sociology. The fact that psychoanalysis in its classic form is inherently ahistorical and is characterized by a radical devaluation of the external world are only the most evident reasons for this.

[1] The systematic use of psychoanalytic theory by historians and sociologists raises the question of the relationship of therapy to theory. Psychoanalysts tend to insist that this kind of work cannot be successfully undertaken unless the researcher has undergone personal analysis. Sometimes psychoanalysts say even more than this. For example, "It is my contention that the psychoanalytic anthropic researcher not only needs full clinical training—such as two or three supervised analyses that students customarily carry out, in the fulfillment of present training programs, before graduation from an institute—but also that he has to have the opportunity for continuous clinical work, if he is to live up to the requirements of his task." Kurt R. Eissler, *Medical Orthodoxy and the Future of Psychoanalysis* (New York, 1965), p. 164. Erikson, however, has said that "we must presuppose that the psychohistorian will have developed or acquired a certain self-analytical capacity which would give to his dealing with others, great or small, both the charity of identification and a reasonably good conscience." "On the Nature of Psychohistorical Evidence: In Search of Gandhi," *Daedalus*, 97 (Summer, 1968): 709. Our own opinion is that the body of theory exists for anyone to use. Neither personal analysis nor clinical training is a guarantee of superior insight. Indeed, see the critique of Eissler's own biographical work by Joseph T. Coltrera, "On the Creation of Beauty and Thought: The Unique as Vicissitude, "*Journal of the American Psychoanalytic Association*, 13, no. 3 (July, 1965): 634–703 (hereafter cited as *J. Amer. Psychoanal. Ass.*). We must also note the following remark from a review of Paul Roazen's *Brother Animal* (New York, 1969). "On one hand, one wonders at how a nonpsychoanalyst is able to utilize analytic concepts with facility; this occurs so frequently that one might doubt the necessity for formal education in psychoanalysis. On the other hand, Roazen's clinical formulations are lacking in the precise observation and detail that bring a clinical report to life; sadly enough, this is also true of the reports of many psychoanalysts." Murray Sherman, "Book Reviews," *Psychoanalytic Review*, 57, no. 3 (1970): 519–20 (hereafter cited as *Psychoanal. Rev.*).

Freud, of course, undertook to interpret man's past and to explain the nature of social organization. Basically, he held two views on these subjects. One, rather elaborately worked out, is based on instinct theory, and represents what we refer to as the classic psychoanalytic approach. The second, far more sociological in implication, is only very rudimentary in form. The problems raised by the first approach, and the suggestions offered by the second, have led subsequent writers to attempt to refine the psychoanalytic approach, and especially to make the theory more tractable in terms of historical and sociological data. Thus, one can find in the literature quite a number of basically psychoanalytic frames of reference. But each of these can in turn be shown to be inadequate on theoretical and methodological grounds—and, hence, ultimately on substantive grounds as well. This, then, presents us with a twofold problem: first, to explain— at least briefly—the shortcomings in certain representative viewpoints; and, second, to organize and explain the merits of an alternative view.

On the basis of his early and rather remarkable discoveries Freud became convinced that psychoanalysis would prove to be the discipline that could master the complexities of culture and history, the one body of knowledge that could outflank and dominate all other approaches to reality—with the exception of art—because it had the capacity to identify and explain the most fundamental aspects of reality. What Freud had identified in clinical experience as determinants of neurosis he translated into social terms as determinants of social organization. Just as the Oedipus complex is the nuclear complex of neurosis, and repressed infantile sexuality is the chief motive force in the formation of symptoms, so these psychic conflicts are played out and reflected in activities in the larger world. The oedipal conflict and the various possible resolutions of that conflict represent the essential substance of external as well as internal reality.

This psychoanalytic standpoint purported to explain man's relationship to the external world (social organization, morality, religion) historically and comparatively in terms of one unchanging psychic reality, the resolution of one overarching and immortal wish, the (simultaneously incestuous and patricidal) wish of the son to displace the father and enjoy exclusive possession of the mother. Society, in these terms, has evolved on the basis of repression, renunciation, and sublimation, as a defense against the fulfillment of the wish; society is based on the existence of the common impulse, which must be controlled if man is to achieve any kind of stable organization.

Moreover, this relationship to external reality was understood to be a matter of phylogenetic inheritance: the story of the primal murder of the father (*Totem and Taboo*) was related as a real, concrete, historical event, the consequences of which were genetically transmitted (i.e., in the Lamarckian sense that acquired characteristics are inherited). Thus, the oedipal drama is inevitably and immutably the decisive reality, and what is important in and for man occurs independently of specific social structures and without reference to historical time.[2] Instinctual life, not the external world and its various manifestations, is understood to be the primary problem.[3]

Freud, therefore, did not see the necessity for systematically investigating the problem of social structure. This traditional psychoanalytic position paid hardly any attention at all to those economic and political structures that historians and sociologists typically regard as significantly determinative of man's life in society. Freud stressed the essentially unchanging content of human wishes rather than the "apparently" changing form of institutions and practices. In the context thus organized, social change is dealt with in terms of the return to consciousness of the repressed oedipal contents, more or less distorted and expressed in a variety of ways. The return of such oedipal contents may lead to attacks against authority, but, because of the need to keep repressed the underlying erotic reality, authority is inevitably restored. "In psychological terms, he [Freud] insisted, there was no change. Society, as a psychological aggregate, was what it had always been. Freud the social theorist, so far as he depended upon Freud the natural scientist, showed the traditional positivist eagerness to eliminate the challenge of history by finding lawfulness in nature."[4]

[2] Freud wrote that the tragedy of Oedipus has universal appeal because his fate might have been our own, "because the oracle laid upon us before our birth the very curse which rested upon him." Further, "Fate and the oracle were no more than the materialization of an internal necessity." Sigmund Freud, "An Autobiographical Study," *The Standard Edition of the Complete Works of Sigmund Freud*, trans. and ed. James Strachey, vol. 20 (London, 1958), p. 63 (hereafter cited by title of the work, volume number, and page).

[3] It should be understood that, when Freud spoke of instinct, instinctual life, or drives, he had in mind an essentially psychological, not a biological, concept. There are, of course, biological and physiological substructures, but the basic thrust of the concept for theory is psychological. In no case should the word be confused with its use in biology and related fields. See Heinz Hartmann, "Psychoanalysis as a Scientific Theory" and "Comments on the Psychoanalytic Theory of Instinctual Drives," *Essays on Ego Psychology: Selected Problems in Psychoanalytic Theory* (New York, 1965), pp. 326–27, 69–89 (hereafter cited as *Essays*). See also the interesting and important contribution by Hans W. Loewald, "On Motivation and Instinct Theory," *Psychoanalytic Study of the Child*, 26 (1971): 91–128 (hereafter cited as *Psychoanal. Stud. Child*).

[4] Philip Rieff, "Psychoanalysis," in *American History and the Social Sciences*, ed. E. Saveth (New York, 1964), p. 119. For an orthodox statement on political authority and the problem of change, see Marie Bonaparte, "Psychoanalysis, Anthropology, and Sociology," in *Psychoanalysis and Culture*, ed. G. B. Wilbur and W. Muensterberger (New York, 1967), p. 148.

Cultural and social beliefs and institutions represent, in this view, a collective defense against the gratification of erotic and aggressive wishes, which are repressed, sublimated, and displaced. Immediate and direct gratification cannot be realized, because this involves the erotic and aggressive apprehension of primal figures. For this reason man directs his attention to, and is bidden to seek, fulfillment in the external world; and he is forever tied to renunciation and deprivation, which are formally imposed by coercive structures and internalized morality. Society is the means by which individuals separate and protect themselves from id demands. The evolution of culture and social structure "permits further projection of control and repressive strivings into larger and more structured collectivities. The essential feature of society—the exogamous family, clan differentiation, hierarchical social structure, political institutions and religion—are all collective responses to the anxiety created by . . . instinctual ambivalence and the tendency to control it through the projection of mythic constructs."[5]

This view of man and of social structure has proven to be a persuasive one. There are evident shortcomings, but to many these do not contradict Freud's essential insight. Some writers have tried to improve on Freud's position while still retaining the fundamental spirit of his critique. Such writers, in brief, continue to view the basic reality as internal and erotic while viewing external structures as a projective screen and a series of defensive techniques. If Freud's position is clarified in order to adjust to biological and historical realities, it will take the form, for example, of abandoning the phylogenetic assumptions, which are at present untenable and about which Freud was ambivalent anyway.[6]

Thus, Geza Roheim attempted to explain social change—which obviously must be accounted for—in these terms: "Culture has authorized and socialized a specific sublimation of reaction-formation and can therefore canalize the latent conflicts of its members in a decreasing proportion. Those who have other emotional needs will introduce cultural modifications. As all human beings consist of a bundle of id-trends and defense mechanisms and as culture provides a sublimation for only some of these, the others, not being thus satiated, will grow in momentum and provide the psychic background in the group which makes the reform movement possible." Roheim, in other words, tried to get around Freud's

---

[5] B. J. Bergen and S. D. Rosenberg, "The New Neo-Freudians: Psychoanalytic Dimensions of Social Change," *Psychiatry*, 34, no. 1 (1971): 31.

[6] See Freud, *Totem and Taboo*, 13: 159–60; see also Derek Freeman, "Totem and Taboo: A Reappraisal," in *Man and His Culture: Psychoanalytic Anthropology after "Totem and Taboo*," ed. W. Muensterberger (London, 1969), pp. 53–78.

notion of phylogenetic inheritance and to explain social change and the varied conditions of different societies on the basis of infantile experiences which happen to occur, which are sublimated but cannot be integrated by the extant social organization, and which have a general appeal because presumably others have the same type of experience, and so forth.

But this explanation raises more questions than it answers. If social change stems from the unsatisfied emotional needs of particular individuals, *how* can action ever become concerted social action—or, why should the psychosexual needs of individuals, which are otherwise disparate (i.e., which are either not the same or are not experienced with the same degree of intensity), merge to produce systematic social action? On what basis are the emotional aspirations of individuals codified, cathected, and acted upon by a group? The inability to use the phylogenetic argument and the insistence that the fundamental reality is internal (or, to say it the other way, the rejection of the possibility of any independent influence of social structure on personality) lead inevitably to reductionist conclusions, and the most significant social events are understood to result from the random infantile experiences of random individuals. If we ask where the diverse emotional contents that cannot be accommodated came from, the answer must be "simply [from] the accidental factors that have always been traumatic for the human infant—death, sexual assaults, aggression, sibling rivalries and other factors not necessarily systematically related to any environmental or cultural situations."[7]

It seems clear, however, that Freud himself was not altogether satisfied with this level of analysis as far as he had taken it. This dissatisfaction is manifest in his major revision of theory, which shifted the emphasis from the repressed to the repressing forces, from id to ego, from libido theory[8] to object relationships, and from internal to external reality. Freud's formulation of structural theory (*The Ego and the Id*, 1923) brings to immediate attention the role played by external objects (via internalization and

[7] Geza Roheim's quote is from "The Psychoanalytic Interpretation of Culture," in *Man and His Culture*, ed. Muensterberger, pp. 40–41. The quote on "accidental factors," is from G. W. Domhoff, "Historical Materialism, Cultural Determinism, and the Origin of the Ruling Class," *Psychoanal. Rev.*, 56, no. 2 (1969): 274. See also, by the same author, "Two Luthers," *ibid.*, 57, no. 1 (1970). For a comprehensive overview of Freud's basic position and various modifications of it, see Bergen and Rosenberg, "The New Neo-Freudians."

[8] "Libido theory" refers to the theoretical description of the universal maturational sequence of stages of sexual development—i.e., oral, anal, phallic, genital. No satisfactory short definition of this aspect of psychoanalysis is possible. The reader is referred to H. Nagera, ed., *Basic Psychoanalytic Concepts on the Libido Theory*, Hampstead Clinic Psychoanalytic Library, vol. 1 (New York, 1969); and Richard Sterba, *Introduction to the Psychoanalytic Theory of the Libido*, 3d ed. (New York, 1968).

identification) in the formation of ego and superego.[9] Henceforth, the relationship of the individual to the love object is the most important factor, determining as it does the character of ego and superego. The formation and development of psychic structure after this are understood to be contingent upon the quality of object relationships.

These and a number of allied suggestions have great sociological import. We may easily infer from this position that social demands, mediated by parental influences, determine to a great degree the development of morality and ideals, modes of adaptation, of work and the mastery of skills, as well as the content of the repressed. The superego certainly develops on the basis of experiences in the external world, especially in contact with parents. But ego, too, is shaped by the individual's relationship to objects. Hence, Freud arrived at one of his last major conclusions: "We have repeatedly had to insist on the fact that ego owes its origins as well as the most important of its acquired characteristics to its relation to the real external world."[10] There is much more to be said on the problem of cultural influences on personality at all levels, and we shall return to this later.

That libido theory alone was not going to carry Freud very far, especially in the explanation of social phenomena, was already clear in *Group Psychology and the Analysis of the Ego*. Freud observed in this work that the psychoanalytic study of neuroses had focused almost exclusively on the libidinal impulses that pursue a sexual aim. In groups, however, this cannot be a central issue, and psychoanalysts had already observed phenomena which represent a diversion of the instinct from its sexual aim. "But we should also like to know whether this kind of object-cathexis, as we know it in sexual life, represents the only manner of emotional tie with other people, or whether we must take other mechanisms of the sort into account. As a matter of fact we learn from psychoanalysis that there do exist other mechanisms for emotional ties, the so called identifications."[11]

---

[9] Psychoanalytic structural theory refers to Freud's organization of the substructures of personality, the id, the ego, and the superego, "which are defined as units of functions. The id refers to the instinctual aspect, the ego to the reality principle and to the 'centralization of functional control' (to borrow a term from brain physiology). The superego has its biological roots in the long dependency on the parents and in the helplessness of the human child; it develops out of identifications with the parents; and it accounts for the fact that moral conflict and guilt feelings become a natural and fundamental aspect of human behavior. The structural formulations, referring to the distinction of ego, id, superego, have several theoretical and clinical advantages. The most important is probably that the demarcation lines of the three systems, ego, id, superego, are geared to the typical conflicts of man: conflicts with the instinctual drives, with moral conscience, and with the outside world." Hartmann, "Psychoanalysis as a Scientific Theory," p. 325.

[10] Freud, "An Outline of Psychoanalysis," 23: 201.

[11] Freud, "Group Psychology and the Analysis of the Ego," 18: 103–4.

However, this particular attempt of Freud's to deal with mass psychology was concerned in effect with crowd behavior, which is typically characterized by an impulsive, emotional, uncontrolled quality, and by regressive identification with a leader, who then supplies control from the outside. Freud did not deal with those social situations which provide the individual with "opportunities for stable object attachments of various sorts," situations which diminish the possibility for regressive behavior.[12] If events in the external world become chaotic, groups of people will behave in a rigid and violent way in order to bring the world back under control. But this is only one possibility, and it is also necessary to account for temporary situations of instability in terms of "regression in the service of the ego," for stable ongoing situations, and for situations of change which are not characterized predominantly by regressive behavior but which rather demonstrate ego and superego control. In Freud's work at this level there is no sense of control over social situations or of the dominance of ego.

Moreover, Freud did not follow up his suggestion with regard to identification, although he extended his sociological position in *Civilization and Its Discontents* along other lines. The emphasis here, on internalized aggression, superego, and guilt—from which we may infer that violations of internalized morality, as this may occur in revolutions, will lead to distorted behavior—is still inadequate on the grounds noted above. It cannot encompass social activity in other than regressive terms. But, more important, it is inadequate even to explain the range of regressive phenomena we have to account for. The rudimentary nature of Freud's concept of object relationships and his reluctance to deal with the external world, to take social reality (beyond the family) seriously, inhibited insight in another direction. We take for granted the decisive role played by external traumatic events, such as economic depression, war, invasion, famine, and the like. However, in psychoanalytic terms such events have quite specific implications; they threaten narcissistic integrity, self-esteem, and—to use Erikson's phrase—identity. That is, the fundamental problem is not drive expression from within (Freud's primary concern) but assault on the stability of personality from without; and the struggle at this level is not against onerous reality but against the loss of this reality, or against the loss of a sense of integration with the world. The response to such a situation is not characterized by fear o he wrath of

[12] See, e.g., Neil J. Smelser, "Social and Psychological Dimensions of Collective Behavior," *Essays in Sociological Explanation* (Englewood Cliffs, N.J., 1968), pp. 106–8. See also F. Neumann, *The Democratic and Authoritarian State: Essays in Political and Legal Theory* (New York, 1957), p. 292.

superego but by fear of abandonment, ego dissolution, and emotional annihilation.[13]

In Freud's work, then, there are essentially two models for the analysis of historical and social events. One, well worked out, stresses primarily libido theory and internal dynamics; behavior is conceived of as independent of external social reality. The second implicates the external world, but for the most part not beyond the level of the family and not in a systematic way. The emphasis in Freud's social thought, in any event, is on internal reality and even, as in *Civilization and Its Discontents*, on the dominance of the phylogenetic inheritance. Moreover, a number of things have followed from this which have not only hampered analysis but which have also interfered with the systematic integration of psychoanalysis in other disciplines.[14] First, all behavior examined in the context Freud presents must be interpreted as regressive behavior; and, second, all

[13] In technical terms, there are *two* origins of character distortion. One, like the transference neuroses, is determined genetically by the vicissitudes in psychosexual development and by the intensity of intrapsychic (id-ego-superego) conflict. The second follows the genetic pattern of the narcissistic neuroses. In this case the vicissitudes that have been most fateful have occurred largely in relation to external objects, and the most intense conflict has been between ego and reality. Freud was aware of this distinction, but he never pursued the implications in his analysis of social problems. The distinction allows us to interpret a wider variety of regressive behaviors and to be more specific about them. See Maxwell Gitelson, "On Ego Distortion," *International Journal of Psychoanalysis*, 38 (1958): 247 (hereafter cited as *Int. J. Psychoanal.*). The problem outlined here also underscores the importance of the question of guilt and shame. It is well understood in the psychoanalytic literature that guilt has been far more extensively studied than shame, and this is amply reflected in historical analyses which typically refer to, or comment on, guilt. On this see Helen B. Lewis, *Shame and Guilt in Neurosis* (New York, 1971), pp. 18–23. In brief, fear of loss of status and position, anxiety over failure to achieve, and loss of pride are closely related to shame sanctions. Guilt stems from the interpretation of loss as the fulfillment of a wish, from the transgression of morality, and so forth. "Whereas guilt is generated whenever a boundary (set by the superego) is touched or transgressed, shame occurs when a goal (presented by the ego ideal) is not being reached. . . . Guilt anxiety accompanies transgression, shame, failure." Further, "If shame can reach such a degree that it appears as conscious anxiety it must imply a severe unconscious threat to the ego. This threat, however, is not the fear of the wrath of the parental images, or in other words, fear of annihilation or mutilation proffered as punishment by the superego under the talion principle. Behind the feeling of shame stands not the fear of hatred, but the fear of *contempt*, which, on an even deeper level of the unconscious, spells fear of *abandonment*, the death by emotional starvation." G. Piers and M. B. Singer, *Shame and Guilt* (Springfield, Ill., 1953), pp. 11, 16. More can be said on this in a variety of connections. See, e.g., nn. 21 and 29 below.

[14] Psychoanalysis has been criticized on a number of grounds, including the above. There is no point in repeating here what must be familiar to many. All that needs to be said at this point is that we may expect from psychoanalytically oriented historical or sociological analyses, based as they must be on empirical observation, what we expect from any other type of analysis: proximal inferences, plausibility, parsimony, and the establishment of a basis for further useful investigation.

attacks against authority must appear to be "illegitimate" attacks, attacks based on the eruption of instinctual forces and not on responses to real events in the external world. In terms of symbolic father-son conflict it is always the son who violates morality and who appears, in this sense, to be the usurper of established authority.[15]

A third model was developed by the authors of the Authoritarian Personality studies. These social-psychological studies were originally directed to the investigation of ethnic prejudice in relation to a general syndrome of intolerant attitudes. Since several of the important researchers on this project had fled Europe to escape fascism, the larger political issues were, of course, always present in their thinking. It is not surprising, therefore, that in the end the political questions were made explicit, and different forms of intolerance as expressions of a particular personality type were related to broader social structural factors.[16]

Two aspects of these studies are of interest here. First, the syndrome that "stands out" in these studies, the one which comes closest to the overall picture of the high scorer (e.g., on the scale devised to measure ethnocentricity), follows the "classic psychoanalytic pattern involving a sadomasochistic resolution of the Oedipus complex," delineated by Erich Fromm as the sadomasochistic character.[17] In brief, this individual

[15] David Bakan has suggested that, historically, just the reverse of this situation obtains, that the father has continuously attempted to destroy the son. The assumption that society and culture serve a predominantly repressive purpose forces the analyst to put the onus on one or the other of the combatants. Either the son wishes to overthrow the father, who is deemed to be the legitimate representative of the extant morality, or the father wishes to suppress the son's aspirations for change or for a share of authority, and so forth. Neither of these two viewpoints is particularly central to our work, and it is possible, in symbolic terms and in a sociohistorical context, that both could occur. See Bakan, *Slaughter of the Innocents* (San Francisco, 1971).

[16] The original study on the authoritarian personality was published in 1950 (T. W. Adorno, Else Frenkel-Brunswik, Daniel J. Levinson, and R. Nevitt Sanford, *The Authoritarian Personality* [New York]); it has recently been reissued in paperback (New York, 1969). A substantial body of literature emerged in response to the original work. For an overview of this literature, see J. Kirscht and R. C. Dillehay, *Dimensions of Authoritarianism: A Review of Research and Theory* (Lexington, Ky., 1967). On the application of the Authoritarian Personality studies to politics in general, see, e.g., Fred I. Greenstein, "Personality and Political Socialization: The Theories of Authoritarian and Democratic Character," *Annals of the American Academy of Political and Social Science*, 361 (September, 1965): 81–95. The applicability of the Authoritarian Personality studies was extended because, as one of the original authors put it, "these variables are thought to be the chief raw materials out of which practically all authoritarian structures are built." D. J. Levinson and P. E. Huffman, "Traditional Family Ideology and Its Relation to Personality," in *Advancing Psychological Science*, vol. 3: *Research in Developmental, Personality, and Social Psychology*, ed. F. H. Sanford and E. J. Capaldi (Belmont, Calif., 1964), pp. 61–62. See also Gordon Allport, *The Nature of Prejudice* (Cambridge, Mass., 1954).

[17] Adorno et al., *The Authoritarian Personality*, p. 759.

achieves social adjustment through compliance and subordination; ambivalence is dealt with by the overevaluation of his authorities, on the one hand, and by the devaluation of a socially defined "outgroup," on the other. Such an individual is characterized by rigid, compulsive behavior, the result of an irrational and punitive superego.

The second aspect, which is separated from the first only for analytic purposes, is that this orientation to the world is understood to derive from socialization within a particular family structure, which is characterized by "a tendency toward rigid discipline on the part of the parents, with affection which is conditional . . . i.e., dependent upon approved behavior on the part of the child." The mode of defense which is typically organized to cope with this harsh, threatening parental, and especially paternal discipline is referred to as "identification with the aggressor." This identification with punitive authority, which brings anxiety under control, also leads to the acceptance of clearly defined roles of dominance and submission in interpersonal relations, a willingness to conform to conventional behavior, a lack of spontaneity in behavior (because emotional expression is interpreted as a sign of weakness and because aggression, which might be aimed at authority, must be kept under control), and to reaction to conflict and diversity in highly indignant, rigidly moral tones.[18]

In such a family situation, in other words, the anxious child signals by his actions a feeling which may be translated as "I'll be like you if you love me." Love for the mother and hatred for the father are repressed, and submission to, and identification with, punitive authority is the means of avoiding punishment and rejection. The hatred felt is turned outward, is readily expressed against all those who seem to represent what one must deny in oneself; at the same time an unreflected glorification and idealization of parental figures is expressed.

Thus, a particular form of socialization is responsible for the development of a particular personality type, one to whom fascist alternatives will or might have a great appeal. However, Herbert Marcuse, who came out of the same intellectual and institutional milieu as T. W. Adorno, the leading figure in the Authoritarian Personality studies, subsequently concluded that the type of personality which is amenable to fascism derives not from a rigid, punitive, overcontrolled family, but rather from a family which does not exercise control, or does so only minimally. This lack of familial control occurs because the earlier legitimation of control—specific social functions, especially in the economic order—no longer applies. Earlier, it was through struggle with the father and mother that

[18] *Ibid.*, pp. 482–83; but see also Erik Erikson's analysis in *Childhood and Society*, 2d ed. (New York, 1963), pp. 330–40.

children entered social life with impulses, ideas, and needs that were their own—i.e., internalized. Now, the permissive father hardly presents himself as the representative of harsh reality and thus is neither a source of conflict nor an ideal figure. The father, therefore, no longer shapes the child's economic, emotional, or intellectual future. Rather, the child gets his cues from a variety of external sources and he is manipulated by the experts of the mass media. Such individuals have no internal integrity, they must conform to the authority of others, and hence they present themselves as the potential fascist, the mass man.[19]

The family, of course, is central to both of these views because this is where socialization takes place in its most basic and enduring form. However, a very important implication emerges from the contradictory analyses of Adorno and Marcuse: the so-called authoritarian personality, or, more specifically, the type of person who would support and participate in a totalitarian movement, can come out of *any* family background, most particularly if events at the social level intervene to disrupt in a violent way an "average expectable environment."[20]

The virtue of these analyses as compared with the classic psychoanalytic position is their stress on the intimate relationship of individual and family to the wider economic and political worlds, and their notion that in significant ways familial patterns change in response to changes in the wider world. But we must observe, too, the overevaluation of the familial-ontogenetic framework which leads to a fixed sense of character—very much in the traditional psychoanalytic fashion—and the stress on a specific socialization process which, in light of the observed contradiction, does not do much to illuminate. Further, this model in its turn appears to be applicable only to regressive phenomena.[21]

Another point should be made here in reference to the contradictory positions taken by Adorno and Marcuse. This pertains rather strictly to

[19] Herbert Marcuse, *Eros and Civilization* (New York, 1962), pp. 87–90; Leon Bramson, *The Political Context of Sociology* (Princeton, 1961), pp. 131–39.

[20] In fact, Else Frenkel-Brunswik had already concluded that events in the external world could force a totalitarian conclusion no matter how tolerant the family context. Else Frenkel-Brunswik, "Psychological Aspects of Totalitarianism," in *Totalitarianism*, ed. C. J. Friedrich (New York, 1964), p. 177.

[21] The authors of *The Authoritarian Personality* quite evidently had the Nazis in mind in the organization of their work. But behavior associated with the Nazi experience, based on the inability to manage traumatic events in the external world, implies very strongly an attack on narcissistic integrity and self-esteem, stemming from a normatively perceived failure (or threatened failure) of the environment, and not the fear of superego which is implied in the given model of socialization. Erich Fromm has addressed himself to at least one aspect of the problem in these terms. See Fromm, *The Heart of Man* (New York, 1964), pp. 66–76. There are, however, serious shortcomings in his work.

clinical psychoanalytic endeavor, but because of the methodological problems raised we will comment on it. Psychoanalysts will explain the manifestation of a harsh and punitive superego in terms of identification with a threatening father; they will also explain this as the result of a situation in which there is no father at all. In the latter case no realistic father figure exists to constrain the archaic fantasies of conquest, punishment, and retribution which characterize preoedipal and oedipal children. This insight may have its explanatory uses in clinical situations, but the historian or the sociologist must be wary of a frame of reference in which similar behaviors are explained on the basis of diametrically opposed hypotheses.[22]

Erikson's work provides us with still another model. This one, too, is based on Freud's later structural theory and aims to integrate in a comprehensive way internal reality and social objects (i.e., a psychosocial, as opposed to a psychosexual, emphasis). In this model—as it was employed, for example, in the work on Luther and Gandhi—an innovative or charismatic individual codifies and expresses popular experience in a time of social change, giving the common man a focus, legitimating rebellious behavior, pointing him to new social goals, to the acceptance of a more complex reality, and to greater levels of personal responsibility. This approach quite readily overcomes the earlier psychoanalytic bias, in that all behavior is not interpreted as regressive behavior (although Erikson certainly addresses himself to this possibility); rather, novel, progressive action is stressed, as the leading individual weaves together different personal and social strands to create a new fabric.

Erikson's contribution is a very important one, and we shall have more to say about his work later on. In this context we simply want to note that, while Erikson acknowledges the importance of the external world, he does not investigate this aspect of reality very extensively—nor does his theoretical frame of reference systematically encompass it. Thus, his emphasis is still typically on the unique individual. Because traditional psychoanalytic theory—and especially libido theory—is most pertinent to this level of analysis, and because Erikson's work has been very influential as well, what we observe in psychohistorical work to date is almost exclusively the analysis of individual biography. Psychohistorians are concentrating their efforts on the study of elite figures.[23] The history of the

[22] See Jule Nydes, "The Paranoid-Masochistic Character," *Psychoanal. Rev.*, 50 (Summer, 1963): 83–84.

[23] On the psychohistorical study of elite figures, see, e.g., Benjamin Wolman, ed., *The Psychoanalytic Interpretation of History* (New York, 1971). There are three empirical studies in this work: G. Bychowski, "Joseph V. Stalin: Paranoia and the Dictatorship of the Proletariat"; Peter Loewenberg, "Theodore Herzl: A Psychoanalytic Study in

common man or of the mass or group is neglected, and the complex effects of social structure on personality are still seriously underevaluated.

This emphasis on the study of individual lives has had one particularly unfortunate consequence that we must mention. One finds in such work the acceptance of an implicit assumption that, since great men have helped to shape great events, they must have had special experiences and insights, but that the effectiveness of their leadership must also reflect common experiences, especially of an ontogenetic-familial sort. On the basis of this position one often notes that, when the problem of mass behavior is addressed, the motivation for this behavior is simply and mistakenly inferred from the motivation of the leader.

Finally, Erikson has done a great service by systematically organizing a theory of the life cycle which explains the need for individuals to be related to different social structures and to meet with and resolve a variety of personality crises, all through life. This facilitates considerably the organization of a comprehensive sociological position. At the same time, however, Erikson has not drawn out a number of evident implications of his work, the reason being his continued commitment to the ontogenetic-familial model. In the end, Erikson's focus is still down and in rather than up and out. Erikson's theory of developmental stages in the family context has, in our view, hampered his work in important ways, no matter how much it has facilitated it in other respects.

Charismatic Political Leadership"; and Robert G. L. Waite, "Adolf Hitler's Anti-Semitism: A Study in History and Psychoanalysis." Professor Loewenberg has also contributed another study recently, on Himmler ("The Unsuccessful Adolescence of Heinrich Himmler," *American Historical Review*, 76, no. 3 [June, 1971]: 612–41); and Waite has another recent publication on Hitler ("Adolf Hitler's Guilt Feelings: A Study in History and Psychology," *Journal of Interdisciplinary History*, 1, no. 2 [Winter, 1971]: 229–49). See also S. Kakar, *Frederick Taylor: A Study in Personality and Innovation* (Cambridge, Mass., 1970); Anne Jardim, *The First Henry Ford: A Study in Personality and Business Leadership* (Cambridge, Mass., 1970); Arthur Mitzman, *The Iron Cage* (New York, 1970), on Max Weber; R. Binion, *Frau Lou: Nietzsche's Wayward Disciple* (Princeton, 1968); Frank Manuel, *A Portrait of Isaac Newton* (Cambridge, Mass., 1968); and E. Victor Wolfenstein, *The Revolutionary Personality: Lenin, Trotsky, Gandhi* (Princeton, 1967). At another level, see Alain Besançon, *Le Tsarèvitch Immolè* (Paris, 1967). Much of this work, though certainly not all of it, is indebted to Erikson's contributions, and Erikson himself has written at one time or another on Gorky, Hitler, Shaw, Luther, and Gandhi. A look at the *Daedalus* issue, "Philosophers and Kings: Studies in Leadership," Summer, 1968, particularly at articles by Bruce Mazlish ("James Mill and the Utilitarians") and Cushing Strout ("William James and the Twice-Born Sick Soul") will serve to point to other work underway. Historians have attempted work with a sociological content (e.g., David Hunt, *Parents and Children in History* [New York, 1970]; Peter Loewenberg, "The Psychohistorical Origins of the Nazi Youth Cohort," *American Historical Review*, 76, no. 5 [December, 1971]: 1457–1502). But the main thrust is certainly in the direction we have indicated.

The last psychoanalytically based frame of reference that we want to consider may be referred to as the generational model. This model is much more explicitly sociological than the others, for it leads to the systematic investigation of a variety of events in the external world and is capable of usefully dealing with a variety of macro (i.e., demographic) data. Briefly, one investigates in these terms what happens to the members of a generation in the decisive period of character development—early childhood—in relation to a significant historical experience which is both shared in common and difficult to master or to assimilate in personality. The emphasis, then, is on fixation points and on regressive modes of defense, because any subsequent traumatic event will be responded to in terms of the defenses originally elaborated. By examining real events in a demographic sense (e.g., changing patterns of work, epidemic, famine, etc.) in the childhood situation, one can understand the types of consolation sought in later situations, especially with regard to the type of leadership which will be sought and accepted.[24]

The difficulty with the generational model in its psychoanalytic form is that it must refer to a birth cohort in order to make sense; it must refer to a similar childhood experience. The modes of behavior have to be established in common so that later responses will exhibit reasonably common features. But one can readily demonstrate in specific instances that adults who are *not* of the same birth cohort respond in a similar way to a given crisis, and that adults who are of the same cohort and who did share a traumatic experience in childhood behave in different ways later on. A comprehensive frame of reference should be capable of readily assimilating these types of data. Therefore, to give an example, even if one could demonstrate that 50–60 percent of a birth cohort subsequently engaged in a similar type of activity, one would still have to account for the remainder and explain why they did not participate. This could be done in an ad hoc or idiosyncratic manner, but theoretical parsimony dictates a unity of explanation for all segments of a cohort. This suggests approaching the problem with some other, more universal set of propositions.[25]

[24] See Loewenberg, "The Psychohistorical Origins of the Nazi Youth Cohort"; on cohort analysis and the socialization process in other circumstances, see *ibid.*, p. 1467, n. 20.

[25] It is possible to organize other logical and empirical combinations. The two possibilities noted, however, should suffice to illustrate the type of question we wish to raise regarding this generational model. On this problem one should also see Abram Kardiner, *The Individual and His Society: The Psychodynamics of Primitive Social Organization* (New York, 1939); and Abram Kardiner *et al.*, *The Psychological Frontiers of Society* (New York, 1945).

We have explained this model in terms of traumatic experience because it is more easily established in these terms. It is applicable, however, to nontraumatic experience as well, simply at the level of socialization. But the same objection can once again be raised. In any case, the model presents too many difficulties; it requires too many logical leaps, and too many inferences have to be made to get from one point (early childhood in a family context) to another point, years later, when people are acting in concert against another or many other institutional structures.

We have now examined five psychoanalytic approaches to historical and sociological data.[26] One is based on the motivating power of drives that are understood to be universal constants. The other four are tied to an ontogenetic-familial scheme which in turn ties the individual to particular societies and circumstances through socialization in the family. However, as useful as this scheme may be clinically in explaining individual dynamics, it inhibits analysis of social-structural events and of group behavior. Thus, while psychosocial studies have acquired a measure of legitimacy in historical and sociological terms, very few questions have been answered, and these mostly in reference to biographical work.

The next step is therefore clear. It is to make use of psychoanalytic propositions, but not in the established way. More specifically, what we want to do here is address ourselves to the *theoretical* issues that are raised by relating psychoanalysis to sociology and to history; to show at an abstract level what is legitimate inference and what is not; to relate external reality to internal dynamics in such a way as to overcome the ahistorical bias in psychoanalysis; to integrate in a systematic frame of reference ego-oriented, relatively controlled behavior with rigid, violent, regressive behavior; to deal in a consistent way with both the social and psychic levels of reality without reducing one to the other—that is, without conceiving of social structure as merely a function of wish, fantasy, and projection and without eliminating the unique idiosyncratic features of personality or of single historical events. Above all, we want to organize a frame of reference that can deal in psychosocial terms with mass and group phenomena as well as with individual behavior.

In doing this we will rely heavily on psychoanalytic propositions, but we will emphasize those aspects of the theory which are either inherently sociological or are more amenable to sociological definition. Thus, we will

[26] These are by no means the only examples of psychoanalytically based models. We could also have referred, for example, to Everett Hagen, *On the Theory of Social Change* (Homewood, Ill., 1962); or to Anthony F. C. Wallace, *Culture and Personality* (New York, 1961). But none of this would have added much to the description of general orientations identified above.

stress the theory of object relations more heavily than the classic libido theory. This means in particular that, no matter how each person is affected by the internal patterns of impulse, conflict, and defense, in the larger sense personality is built up and organized on the bases of identification with, and internalization of, patterns of behavior transmitted by emotionally significant figures.[27] These figures have a temporal priority which enables them to impress on the individual the effective subsequent priority of symbolic codes. The emphasis, therefore, is on the cultural meaning of objects and, simultaneously, on the consequences of object relatedness, object constancy, affective exchange, standards of interpretation and evaluation, and factors of this order. Without this shift in emphasis there can be no sociologically grounded psychoanalysis and hence no psychoanalytic investigation of groups.

Following from this we will also stress symbolic meanings rather than real object ties.[28] The particular, specific object relationship is relevant to clinical work, but not to historical (with the exception of biographical) or sociological work. We are interested in individuals and groups in particular cultural and social settings, and in how they wish or expect to be treated. Thus, we will focus on culturally and socially defined standards and expectations (referring, e.g., to political commitments, work processes, forms of familial organization, of scientific pursuit, religious devotion, and the like) in psychosocial terms of internalization and object relationships—that is, on the ramifications involved in continued attachment to, or loss of (the inability to manage goal-directed behavior in terms of), such standards.

We will also insist that personality is not so rigidly fixed in earlier years—with the resolution of oedipal conflict or even with the resolution of adolescent and identity crises—as the more traditional psychoanalytic view has it. What we want to show is that *any* network of object relationships constitutes a context of psychic support and gives meaning to situations, and that identity is comprised of such relationships.[29] The loss of an object in its expectational content and context means the loss of psychic support and a threat to identity, and this must lead to one or another type of behavior, from apathy, depression, and withdrawal, on one side, to a greater sense of liberation and capacity for autonomy, on the other. That is, failure of symbolic codes, the inability to act on internalized standards and expectations, for whatever structural reasons, can dynami-

[27] Hans Gerth and C. Wright Mills, *Character and Social Structure: The Psychology of Social Institutions* (New York, 1953).
[28] Mary Douglas, "Deciphering a Meal," *Daedalus* (Winter, 1972): 61–81.
[29] Helen M. Lynd, *On Shame and the Search for Identity* (New York, 1958).

cally affect classes or groups of people *at all levels of the personality and at any point in the life cycle*, thereby producing a variety of collective behaviors. Moreover, there is no implication in this that such behaviors will necessarily assume a regressive form; rather, new identities and new institutional structures can be forged in such situations.

It should be clear at the outset that we understand the various psychic levels to be in themselves "action" systems. By this we mean that psychic processes at all levels of personality interact with one another but are also in "direct exchange" with culture and society, on the one hand, and with organic processes, on the other. However, society establishes the possibility for ongoing action in terms of specific (internalized) mandates, so that personal stability depends to the greatest degree upon the continued integrity of the social order. This is meant to imply further that no substantial part of the personality (e.g., the id) is unavailable to socialization. All levels of personality are structured by the particular standards of the society in which people live—formal or informal, morally appropriate or not. This situation leads to the shared experience of loss and to the possibility for concerted action when symbol systems are violated or are otherwise experienced as having failed.

A stable ongoing structure leads to characteristic types of functions—that is, to modes of perception, of cognitive and social behavior, to choice of defenses, and generally to the organization of self in a pattern of congruent behavior. The repudiation of these functions—if this is to eventuate in concerted action, no matter how regressed it may be—depends upon the internalization of an alternative morality. However, because commitments to morality and ideals are not always conscious they are not always available for criticism on the basis of cognitive processes. Thus, we intend to emphasize affective behavior in particular as a dependent variable. And, while we are interested in affective behavior at the level of the individual, we are more concerned with obligated expressions of emotion which exist as the basis of exchange and integration at the social level, binding people to each other and to larger collectivities while in turn providing individuals with a personal sense of group solidarity and stability.[30]

The two processes we have referred to so far, internalization and object loss, provide the basis for investigation of situations of stability and

---

[30] It must be noted, however, that in any systematic change at the social and personal levels patterns other than the affective must change. That is, changes in affective commitments mean change simultaneously in ways of categorizing and integrating persons and institutions and changes in ways of evaluating and sanctioning behavior. See F. Weinstein and G. M. Platt, *The Wish To Be Free* (Berkeley and Los Angeles, 1970), chap. 1.

change. However, as far as we have been able to go, this frame of reference is particularly applicable to activity at the political, familial, and personal levels. This is especially true of our model of radical change, which really refers to revolutionary situations. There are obviously other forms of social change which have similar impact, such as urbanization, immigration, and the like, and there are other institutional levels at which social change affects psychic responses to a similar extent—as with changes in work processes due to industrialization. But we cannot yet address ourselves to all of these manifestations, although we can explain a variety of known responses to these types of change.[31]

We will, then, orient psychoanalytic insight to a systematic sociological position.[32] In part we find justification for this in the later writings of Freud himself. This view is further supported by Erikson's work on the psychoanalytic side, and by the tradition of normative sociology as exemplified in the work of such writers as Durkheim, Weber, Parsons, and others. But we want to state categorically that it is also supported by the emphasis which has consistently been manifest in the psychoanalytic literature as it has developed over the last quarter-century. There is no explicitly formulated sociological position in this literature, but there is clearly an implicit emergent one. We refer here to the very general type of psychoanalytic contribution as this appears in the journal literature. It is not at all hard to find in psychoanalytic discussions questions and statements of a sociological sort.

This development stems from two different but related sources. On one level, psychoanalysts had realized by the late 1930s that there were serious gaps in the theory, that as an explanatory tool the theory was incomplete in important respects but particularly in terms of object relations and the individual's ties—via identification and internalization—with the social world. At the same time, Freud's development of the structural theory pointed specifically in this direction and provided the legitimation for such work and the frame of reference within which it could be carried on. Thus, "while earlier psychoanalytic contributions emphasized genetic, instinctual and intrapsychic processes, the intro-

---

[31] Edward Shorter has attempted to demonstrate that our framework has wider applicability, that is, covers more than revolutionary behavior. He has dealt with reactions to loss in terms of industrialization and urbanization. See Shorter, "Illegitimacy, Sexual Revolution, and Social Change in Modern Europe," *Journal of Interdisciplinary History*, 2 (1971): 237–72, esp. 248ff.

[32] We have addressed ourselves to this problem before, in *The Wish To Be Free*. However, as noted in the preface, with the above formulations and with the propositions we will introduce subsequently, we are withdrawing from certain theoretical positions established in that study, and we will also elaborate in important ways on other positions.

duction of the structural hypothesis, the development of the ego psychology and the newer theory of anxiety opened the way to the further study of the ego's relations with external reality."

At another level, and particularly in that psychoanalysis had shifted its primary location to the United States, problems in therapy which were different from the classical neurotic patterns Freud had earlier treated and described were turning up in a rather systematic way. In brief, "there are vast differences in those who have sought analytic treatment over the years between the early flamboyant hysteric, who has all but disappeared, and the current group, whose conflicts appear to be chiefly in the area of object relationships. If such changing patterns reflect broad psycho-historical processes, the assumptions underlying the model of the psychic apparatus, that one may generalize for the entire species, would have no relevance in this context."

The shortcomings in theory, then, and the different kinds of symptoms and complaints encountered in clinical work converged on the problems of ego, superego, object relationships, and the nature of man's ties to the external world—meaning, specifically, social reality beyond the par- ticular familial relationships Freud might have been concerned with. A number of more recent contributions to theory have facilitated an approach to the problem of social reality; but, in addition, a broader basis for analysis has been established in terms that Freud introduced but never extensively pursued. Thus, Freud pointed out that superego can regress in psychosexual terms—to anal modes in obsessional neurosis and to oral sadistic modes in depression—and in terms of object relations. But, while Freud was more likely to pursue the former problem, the latter one has more recently received the greater degree of attention. This emphasis on object relationships facilitates analysis of attachments to different types of authority figures, and, because of this development, one can observe the shift in psychoanalytic concern with cultural problems which occurred around the mid-1950s, from the analysis of art and artistic endeavor to the analysis of political figures and social movements. In these terms, too, we can understand why the following kind of statement on rebellious be- havior would now appear in the psychoanalytic literature: "Social institutions transcend individual motivations. They help to define be- havioral roles and moral standards, and evoke similar behavior in people of disparate backgrounds. Early childhood experience is only an initial influence among many factors that shape dissident behavior."

The point of this information is that the sociological concern among psychoanalysts is very concentrated, specific, and recurrent. In fact, virtually all of the statements noted immediately above come out of recent editions of the *Journal of the American Psychoanalytic Association*.[33] However, we could have done as much with any of the major psychoanalytic journals.[34] In spite of this, psychoanalysts have not yet addressed themselves to this situation in a systematic way—although many basic psychoanalytic propositions are being called into question—nor have they, to our knowledge, made an attempt to understand where this concern

[33] The first quote (pp. 18–19) is from the panel report "Genetic, Dynamic, and Adaptive Aspects of Dissent," by Robert D. Gillman, *J. Amer. Psychoanal. Ass.*, 19, no. 1 (January, 1971): 122. The second quote (p. 19) is from the panel report "Models of the Psychic Apparatus," by Samuel Abrams, *ibid.*, p. 135. The problem of regression in object relationships is discussed by Burton N. Wixen, "Object-Specific Superego Responses," *ibid.*, 18, no. 4 (October, 1970): 835. The observation that psychoanalytic interest has shifted from art to politics is in John E. Mack, "Psychoanalysis and Historical Biography," *ibid.*, 19, no. 1 (January, 1971): 151. The final quote (p. 19) is again from the Gillman report "Genetic, Dynamic, and Adaptive Aspects of Dissent," *ibid.*, p. 125. See also, e.g., the panel report "Social Deprivation in Childhood and Character Formation," by Jeanne Spurlock, *ibid.*, 18, no. 3 (July, 1970): 622–30.

On the problems as they emerged in theory, see David Rapaport's Introduction to Erikson's *Identity and the Life Cycle*, Psychological Issues, no. 1 (New York, 1959), esp. p. 11. See also Talcott Parsons's treatment of the theoretical problems from a sociological standpoint in *Social Structure and Personality* (Glencoe, Ill., 1964). On the problems as they emerged in therapy, see, e.g., Maxwell Gitelson, "Therapeutic Problems in the Analysis of the 'Normal Candidate,'" *Int. J. Psychoanal.*, 35 (1954): 174–83. In relation to Gitelson's observations, see also Helen Tartakoff, "The Normal Personality in Our Culture and the Nobel Prize Complex," *Psychoanalysis: A General Psychology*, ed. R. M. Loewenstein *et al.* (New York, 1966), pp. 222–52. The following work on this point may also be noted: Heinz Hartmann, "Psychoanalysis and Sociology," *Essays*, p. 26; Anna Freud, "The Mutual Influences in the Development of Ego and Id," *Psychoanal. Stud. Child*, 7 (1952): 50; L. B. Boyer and P. L. Giovacchini, *Psychoanalytic Treatment of Schizophrenic and Characterological Disorders* (New York, 1967), pp. 310–11; F. J. Hacker, "The Discriminatory Function of the Ego," *Int. J. Psychoanal.*, 43 (November–December, 1962): 395–96; H. Nagera, "The Concepts of Structure and Structuralization," *Psychoanal. Stud. Child*, 22 (1967): 95; B. R. Easser and S. R. Lesser, "Hysterical Personality: A Re-evaluation," *Psychoanalytic Quarterly*, 34, no. 3 (1965): 390 (hereafter cited as *Psychoanal. Quart.*).

[34] See, e.g., Anna Maenchen, "On the Techniques of Child Analysis in Relation to Stages of Development," *Psychoanal. Stud. Child*, 25 (1970): 180, n.4; Z. Alexander Aarons, "Normality and Abnormality in Adolescence," *ibid.*, pp. 309–10; Dale R. Meers, "Contributions of a Ghetto Culture to Symptom Formation," *ibid.*, p. 210; Hans W. Loewald, "Psychoanalytic Theory and the Psychoanalytic Process," *ibid.*, pp. 66–67; Seymour L. Lustman, "Cultural Deprivation," *ibid.*, p. 489. See also G. Bychowski, "Psychoanalytic Reflections on the Psychiatry of the Poor," *Int. J. Psychoanal.*, 51 (1970): 503–9; A. Mitscherlich *et al.*, "On Psychoanalysis and Sociology," *ibid.*, pp. 35–44; and A. Mitscherlich, "Psychoanalysis and the Aggression of Large Groups," *ibid.*, 52 (1971): 161–67; and the panel report "Protest and Revolution," *ibid.*, 51 (1970): 211–18. Add further, Joseph Barnett, "Dependency Conflicts in the Young Adult," *Psychoanal. Rev.*, 58, no. 1 (1971): 114; John Halverson, "Amour and Eros in the Middle Ages," *ibid.*, 57, no. 2 (1970): 253; Leo Stone, "The Psychoanalytic Concept of Aggression," *Psychoanal. Quart.*, 40, no. 2 (1971): 227. This represents an illustrative but by no means exhaustive cross section of the literature. Other sociologically oriented questions and statements in the literature will be referred to throughout.

comes from and what it can mean—not only for theory, we might add, but also for clinical work.

There is no need to carry this too far at this point; we will return to the problem later. But there is one more example to which we would like to refer. In the most recent edition of the *Psychoanalytic Study of the Child* Hans Loewald examines the biological and psychological implications of the concepts of instinct and drive. Freud's own work is ambiguous with regard to these terms, although he meant to employ instinct as a psychological concept and not a biological one. In clarifying Freud's meaning, Loewald writes that *"instincts, understood as psychic, motivational, forces, become organized as such through interactions within a psychic field consisting originally of the mother-child (psychic) unit."* Loewald states further that "the neonate's incoherent urges, thrashings, and reflex activities become coordinated *and organized into instincts* and assume aims and direction by activities and responses coming from the environment."[35]

We cannot be too emphatic about the sociological meaning of these statements. Not the least conclusion to be drawn from them is one we have already referred to: culture affects personality at all levels, including the id.[36] At any rate, we can state firmly that the position we take is consistent with psychoanalytic observation and emerges from certain vital aspects of psychoanalytic theory. Thus, we view our work as—at the very least—an anticipation of what must follow in the near future. We can be firm on this because it seems clear to us that this sociological concern is prompted by rather evident effects of social process on personality. That is, not only

[35] Loewald, "On Motivation and Instinct Theory," pp. 118, 120; italics added in the second quote. On Freud's inconsistent use of the term "instinct," see *ibid.*, pp. 109, 126. With regard to the sociological issue, see note 34; see also Samuel Ritvo, "Late Adolescence," *Psychoanal. Stud. Child*, 26 (1971): 241–63, esp. 242. The problems raised by adolescence in this society constitute perhaps the most important impetus for this emerging sociological emphasis. The implications at this stage can hardly be avoided.

[36] Thus, e.g., "The only mental processes that we can observe, the only ones about which we can collect information by the use of psychoanalysis, are ones which have clearly been influenced by experience, ones which have been, in part, molded by observation, by memory, by thought, however primitive; in a word, ones which involve the functioning of the child's ego." This means that, as the unconscious must include *the repressed unconscious*, not only are ego and superego processes affected by the external world, but so too are id processes. Charles Brenner, "The Psychoanalytic Concept of Aggression," *Int. J. Psychoanal.*, 52 (1971): 141. See also Henri Parens and Leon J. Saul, *Dependence in Man* (New York, 1971), pp. 13–53. This work abstracts and focuses on the sociological content in Freud. Parens and Saul simply take for granted that id processes are structured by external influences; for them it is not even a problem. See, e.g., *ibid.*, pp. 39–41. For an interesting exposition of this position, see Roy Schafer, "Ideals, Ego Ideal, and Ideal Self," in *Motives and Thought: Essays in Honor of David Rapaport*, ed. R. R. Holt, Psychological Issues, no. 18/19 (New York, 1967), pp. 131–76, esp. p. 147 and n. 13.

have the problems faced by psychoanalysts changed between Freud's day and our own, but they are changing in directions which follow from specific types of pressures put on people in this society. Consistent examination of the problem here will lead, we believe, to a systematic sociological position.

Such a shift in emphasis will undoubtedly present problems to the thoughtful investigator. For example, it becomes necessary to modify the economic aspect of the psychoanalytic metapsychology in developing a general sociopsychoanalytic theory.[37] The psychoanalytic conception of psychic economics—quantities of energy ascribed to psychic processes employed for a variety of purposes—forces one to the conclusion that libidinal and aggressive drive elements are highly idiosyncratic: no two people cathect objects at the same level of intensity; no one can explain the tenacity or flexibility of libido from person to person; no one can explain the choice of neurosis. Moreover, as far as the theory has gone, such a factor as the severity of superego is still conceived of as dependent as much on each individual's fantasies as on what the parents do or the way that they behave.

Two factors are involved in this. On the one hand, different group and mass behaviors are simply better explained in psychosocial terms. But the literal acceptance of economic propositions would prevent the development of a general theory directed toward the analysis of collective behavior; given the idiosyncratic features we have described, no sociological statement can be justified. On the other hand, terms do have to be em-

---

[37] It should be understood that the economic point of view is seriously questioned by a number of psychoanalysts in any case. See, e.g., R. R. Holt, "Beyond Vitalism and Mechanism: Freud's Concept of Psychic Energy," in *Historical Roots of Contemporary Psychology*, ed. Benjamin Wolman (New York, 1968), pp. 196–226; John Bowlby, *Attachment and Loss*, vol. 1: *Attachment* (New York, 1969), pp. 14–18; the panel report, "The Use of the Economic Viewpoint in Clinical Psychoanalysis," *Int. J. Psychoanal.*, 51 (1970): 245–49; and A. D. Rosenblatt and J. Thickstun, "A Study of the Concept of Psychic Energy," *ibid.*, pp. 265–78. See also Holt, *Motives and Thought*, from which economic propositions are excluded.

A word should also be said on the meaning of psychoanalytic "metapsychology." This is a term "first used by Freud to indicate that the assumptions of psychoanalytic psychology went beyond the scope of conscious experience to explain behavior. It represents the highest level of abstraction in the continuum from clinical observation to psychoanalytic theory, and serves as a conceptual tool for establishing an orienting and systematizing framework around which clinical data and lower-level psychoanalytic propositions can be organized. Since the academic psychology of the late 19th and early 20th century equated 'mental' with 'conscious', unconscious processes were considered outside the realm of the mind and hence 'beyond psychology' (the literal translation of metapsychology)." B. E. Moore and B. D. Fine, eds., *A Glossary of Psychoanalytic Terms and Concepts*, 2d ed. (New York, 1968), p. 61. There is more to be said on this subject, and the reader is referred to this work.

ployed which account for the unique individuality of persons. That is, personality does have idiosyncratic features in relation to its own genetic composition as well as to personal experiences with parents, teachers, friends, and other social objects.[38]

We can resolve this apparent contradiction by assuming that personality is mainly comprised of cultural and social symbols internalized in the socialization process. There are idiosyncratic aspects of personality, but there are also—and more important for our purposes—aspects that are shared, and the symbolic codes on which the sharing is based have a controlling influence over the individual in society. In these terms we can understand how a class of individuals experiences, within a believable latitude, similar erotic and aggressive feelings or inhibitions, or how similar frustrations, fears, and anxieties can arise in a group of people faced with the same social conditions. In any case, no matter how useful and relevant economic propositions are for individual, clinical purposes, for sociological purposes the whole problem must be reconsidered. This may affect one of the important concepts in psychoanalysis, but it is necessary to account for other data and to accommodate other levels of analysis in a parsimonious way; moreover, this position builds a theoretical bridge between individuals and society without reducing one to the other.

The standpoint outlined here must also be viewed in terms of the two most important general categories of sociological analysis. In the broadest terms, one category stresses rationality, consciousness, self and class interest, and understands the ultimate determinant of order to be force; the second stresses the primacy of normative standards in social process, a position which is based on some notion of society as a "moral community" and in which the ultimate determinant of order is compliance. In the latter position coercive force is still a vital factor in analysis, but it does not have priority except under specific social circumstances and in relation to particular institutions (e.g., the political structure). For a variety of reasons we can integrate only discrete elements of the first position in our analysis. And, though we follow the second in outline, it is necessary to take issue with various aspects of that framework as well.

We cannot discuss either of these sociological views at length, but we can abstract certain crucial points in order to underscore the basis of our disagreement. Thus, with regard to the first category, a number of important

---

[38] The economic point of view, which ascribes to psychic processes energies independent of somatic sources, raises the question of mind-body dualism, a problem which psychoanalysts would like to resolve. See Rosenblatt and Thickstun, "A Study of the Concept of Psychic Energy," *passim*. It will most likely be possible shortly to work in psychoanalytic theory independently of economic propositions, via cybernetic models, information theory, and so forth.

sociological theories point to an evolutionary, progressive rationalization of psychic and social structures. These theories may refer to rationalization in the sense that personal action is brought under control; or the reference may be to a particular type of social organization in which standards of efficiency (i.e., profit and loss) are applied in the assessment of performance. For example, Mannheim wrote that "the characteristic quality of capitalist bourgeois consciousness is that it knows no bounds to the process of rationalization." And then (following sentiments and fears expressed also by Marx, Weber, Tönnies, and others) he indicated that, "as capitalist organization expands, man is increasingly treated as an abstract calculable magnitude, and tends more and more to experience the outside world in terms of these abstract relations."[39]

One problem that recurs with these theories on rationalization is that the two levels at which rationalization can occur are confused or are not distinguished from each other. But, more important, these theories cannot comprehend the nonconscious bases of such a behavioral style, or the kinds of ambivalence and conflict engendered by it. Rationalization in either sense has never led to action exclusively in terms of conscious self or class interest, nor is it possible for ongoing societies not to fix boundaries for the rationalization process at either level. It is evident that, within the kind of society that Mannheim refers to, and even within highly bureaucratized segments of such a society, very ordinary and prosaic day-to-day activities were continued, activities that were by any standard opposed to, or in violation of, the mandates and norms of rationality.[40] The real actions that people engaged in (e.g., marriage and child-rearing, or the devotion to ideals and authority at the political level) inhibited the extent of the rationalization process at both levels and the predicted consequences never materialized. The kind of sociological frame of reference that Mannheim employed cannot explain this continued commitment to the essentially nonconscious and nonrational aspects of such activities. Psychoanalytic theory, however, can at least provide the basis for such an explanation.[41]

[39] Karl Mannheim, *Essays in Sociology and Social Psychology*, ed. P. Kecskemeti (New York, 1953), pp. 85, 87.

[40] Alfred Schutz, "The Social World and the Theory of Social Action," *Social Research*, 27, No. 2 (1960): 204–21; and Harold Garfinkel, "The Rational Properties of Scientific and Common Sense Activities," *Studies in Ethnomethodology* (Englewood Cliffs, N.J., 1967), pp. 262–83.

[41] Pareto made the same point for behavior at the social level—i.e., that behavior is never totally rational, and that the nature of social life and norms prevents it from becoming so. Vilfredo Pareto, *Mind and Society: A Treatise on General Sociology*, ed. Arthur Livingston, trans. Andrew Bongiorno and Arthur Livingston, vols. 1–3 (New York, 1935).

Marx is undoubtedly the best known among those who employ the first category of analysis, and his work does not require great amplification here. We introduce certain aspects of it briefly in order to note some other reflections of the problem. Marx predicated his work on the assumption of the progressive rationalization of structures, on technologically impelled, changing structural conditions which would eventuate in irreconcilable contradictions at the social level of activity, which in turn would lead to increasingly intense class conflict. In his view these social processes would be characterized by such factors as the de-differentiation of hierarchy and skill among workers as more sophisticated machines took their place, by the progressive impoverishment of the working class, and, of course, by increasing working-class consciousness. However, little that Marx predicted in these terms actually occurred in the advanced industrial societies to which he addressed his work.

One reason for this was that capitalism became more complex and differentiated, changing its form in essential ways, and, in particular, moving from family-based to corporate enterprises, a move which changed the relationship between ownership and control, and so forth. But, not only was Marx unable to see the kind of transition which lay ahead; he could not explain certain social forces that were already extant and operative in the capitalistic societies he knew, forces that were tending to inhibit the kinds of conclusions he insisted were inevitable. It is clear that, because he lacked such a construct as internalization—indeed, any sophisticated awareness of psychic processes in any terms—Marx never could understand why workers in the most advanced industrial societies would not react in the manner he had anticipated.[42] He could not under-

---

[42] The concept of internalization and the related concept of identification are of great importance for historical and sociological work, more important than the concept of superego as such, since internalization and identification go on at other than the superego level. At a later point in this work we will attempt to frame these concepts in a more explicitly sociological fashion. For now, internalization may be defined as follows: "Internalization refers to all those processes by which the subject transforms real or imagined regulatory interactions with his environment, and real or imagined characteristics of his environment, into inner regulations and characteristics." Identification may be defined in this way: "In its fullest sense, the process of identifying with an object is unconscious, though it may also have prominent and significant preconscious and conscious components; in this process the subject modifies his motives and behavior patterns, and the self-representations corresponding to them, in such a way as to experience being like, the same as, and merged with one or more representations of that object; through identification, the subject both represents as his own one or more regulatory influences or characteristics of the object that have become important to him and continues his tie to the object; the subject may wish to bring about this change for various reasons; an identification may acquire relative autonomy from its origins in the subject's relations with dynamically significant objects." The above

stand the levels at which workers (as well as the other elements of society) could become attached to the social order, and, consequently, the reasons for the desire and the ability to organize a trade-union movement, as opposed to a revolutionary movement.[43]

It must be emphasized that Marx wrote in the tradition of cognitive rationality and with a profound commitment to cognitive orientations, to ego-oriented activity, mastery, and control. There is in his work no awareness or appreciation of the processes we now recognize as having interfered with his grand aspirations for man's future. In the Marxist frame of reference there is no way to explain satisfactorily, for example, the very damaging failures of radical politics in the twentieth century. What we are faced with, at least in the European context, is rather a level of violence, a sense of anxiety, and a variety of distortions of reality which are beyond the explanatory power of any sociological view based on interest and consciousness.

Some writers have tried to rectify the evident shortcomings in Marx's work with regard to psychological insight by combining his sociology with

---

quotes are from Roy Schafer, *Aspects of Internalization* (New York, 1968), pp. 9, 140. See also, e.g., Urie Bronfenbrenner, "Freudian Theories of Identification and Their Derivatives," *Child Development*, 31 (1960): 15–40.

Ralf Dahrendorf (*Class and Class Conflict in Industrial Society* [Stanford, Calif., 1959], p. 65) has explained that Marx was sociologically naive to imagine that capitalist societies would be unable to cope with the class conflict generated by its structure. "In fact, every society is capable of coping with whatever new phenomena arise in it, if only by the simple yet effective inertia which can be described . . . as the process of institutionalization." However, the concept of institutionalization is misleading in this context unless it includes the concept of internalization. At one level institutionalization can be consciously apprehended as repetitive and patterned aspects of social life. If institutionalization referred simply to this, such patterns could relatively easily be changed at any time according to the needs or wishes of particular interests. The point is that change is very difficult to achieve, and especially revolutionary change, because the commitments to values are not entirely under conscious control. Dahrendorf indicates that institutionalization began with the process of inclusion in both economic and political spheres. But it was the internalization of these values, not merely their institutionalization, which inhibited conflict in capitalist societies, and it was precisely this kind of process which Marx never could have perceived within his frame of reference.

[43] This is not to say that Marxism has never provided the basis for revolutionary change. In fact, the contrary is true. But the social and psychological processes that characterize Marxist revolutions are at best only partly explicable in Marxist terms. In particular, Marx anticipated that revolution would occur in the context of appropriate cultural conditions, one vital aspect of which was conscious control over reality by the mass of workers. However, Marxist activists in effect set about to seize power, on the assumption that they could create these cultural conditions. It is the failure here, particularly in the Soviet Union in the Stalin era, which cannot be defined or explained in Marxist terms. "Bureaucratic deformation" is hardly an adequate term with which to comprehend the extent and content of Stalin's terror.

aspects of psychoanalytic theory.[44] However, the result of this effort has been the restatement of Marx's vision of the harmonious community in terms of inferior quality. This approach has not led to a more theoretically and empirically sound mode of analysis. A considerable amount of effort has been focused on Marx's concept of alienation, in terms of simplistic characterizations of hierarchical and oppressive authority and its effects on workers and others. The trouble with these discussions of the problem, and the trouble with Marx's original discussion, is that, if this experience of alienation, no matter how the term is defined, continues over a period of time to the extent that Marx and others have imagined, then the result must be a sense of psychic isolation, despair, an inability to identify with self, others, or ideology, and, finally, a condition of apathy and an incapacity to act in a systematic way at all. Alienation as it has been conceived of by Marx and others could never lead to concerted social action.[45] There is a fundamental contradiction in this position which cannot be resolved within the given frame of reference.

The contributions of normative sociology provide a better basis for analysis of the types of data we are interested in, but there are problems with this school as well. Weber's work, to take an example of an important writer in this tradition, also embodies an extraordinary quantity and quality of theoretical and methodological, as well as substantive, materials for the social-scientific analysis of historical data. In fact, Weber's sociology, and particularly his comparative analysis of religion, consisted of studies of historical development and social change. At the same time, these studies were also intended to serve as a critique of Marx's position, and of the assumptions of consciousness and rationality embedded in it. Some of the concepts that Weber contrived and employed, such as "calling" and "charisma," imply commitments and orientations to action which are not entirely under conscious control.

Weber actually organized four categories of action, only one of which was consistent with Marx's category of class interest and expedient rationality. The other three categories of action (i.e., value-rational behavior, as with ascetic religious commitments, and traditional and affective orientations to behavior) are ways of describing motives to action which are not wholly dependent upon rationality and interest. Weber spent a great deal of time working out comparative and evolutionary

[44] Writers have also tried to amplify Marx's position on class conflict to account for the varieties of groups that may become involved in social struggle, groups that cut across class lines such as in the struggle for women's rights or in the student movement.
[45] See G. M. Platt and F. Weinstein, "Alienation and the Problem of Social Action," in *The Phenomenon of Sociology*, ed. Edward Tiryakian (New York, 1971), pp. 284–310.

social-structural models to which he related these categories of action. By doing this he established one means of relating psychic- to social-structural events—although what he meant by this is quite different from what we will outline here, and by contemporary standards must represent only a beginning.

No one can gainsay the value of Weber's contribution. However, there are serious shortcomings in his work, and in this limited context it is necessary for us to focus on them. To begin with, Weber was afraid that the progressive rationalization of social structures was having a deleterious effect on man, and he saw no substantial means of interrupting this process within the given social context. Rationality, according to Weber, was a standard which actors aspired to live up to, and they were obliged and committed to the rationalization of processes on every level. He thought, for example, that the commitment to rationality was affecting other, nonrational modes of expression, including the aesthetic.[46]

In Weber's view, rational and the nonrational (especially religious) commitments had been fused within occupational callings. But he came to see, particularly in the United States, that the religious motivations for work were dissolving, and that what remained were only instrumental concerns. Divested of the ennobling motives of religion, and oriented now ultimately and predominantly to the maximization of profit, work was dehumanizing; hence we have Weber's image of the "iron cage." In this sense Weber accepted Marx's conclusions regarding modern industrial organization, though he disagreed with Marx's logic.

The paramount criterion of this process of rationalization was the development of bureaucracy as the most efficient means of organizing large-scale tasks involving great numbers of people. Bureaucracy had become a universal instrument of social organization, but, once the form had been instituted, it was progressively divorced from any loftier aims and was turned against people, using them solely as instruments for the maximization of ends. Because bureaucracy functioned without regard to institutional goals or ideological commitments, Weber understood it to be as repressive and destructive of man as Marx had earlier understood capitalism to be.

[46] On the cultural level it is possible to trace the increasing importance of cognitive orientations (as opposed to religious, moral, and aesthetic-expressive orientations) from the seventeenth century on—for example, in the emergence and development of modern science. Weber was concerned with this level of analysis and he pointed to the progressive rationalization of Western culture. But this was not as important to him theoretically as was the rationalization and secularization of everyday activity. See, on this, especially Max Weber, *General Economic History*, trans. Frank Knight (New York, 1961).

Moreover, because Weber could see no forces within the system capable of inhibiting this process, and because he was also reluctant to accept the consequences, he had to find a way out. This he did through the concept of the charismatic leader. Charismatic authority had the potential for transforming traditional societies into modern rational-legal societies; but the reverse movement also was possible. Weber conceived of rational-legal systems as inherently problematic, and so the reversal to traditional social forms remained an abiding hope.

There has been a great deal of criticism of Weber's concepts of authority and his rather unidimensional view of bureaucracy.[47] But there are two related aspects of such criticism which must be underscored. First, a sharp distinction must be drawn between the norm of rationality and the possibility of human behavior becoming in fact totally rational. Second, there is still the question of whether modern social organization can be transformed without a return to traditional norms.

One thing is certain: there have always been extant in the West value orientations other than the rational and the cognitive which, as we have noted, have prevented rationalizing tendencies from being realized in an ultimate way. Moreover, recent concern with moral, and especially with aesthetic-expressive, mandates has proved to be rather widespread and has drawn upon these long-standing cultural aspirations.[48] The fate of this concern is far from settled; there is a great deal of resistance to expressive behavior, and so it is impossible to draw any conclusions with regard to possible outcomes. We can conclude, however, that this focus of concern, which has penetrated quite deeply, is not consistent with Weber's idea of interminable bureaucratization.

The point is that ultimate problems of life and existence have never proved amenable to solutions at the level of logic. Moral, ethical, and aesthetic questions have defied rational resolution. It would seem that situational features of life are not entirely open to scientific analysis as far as individuals are concerned as they act in their everyday environment; social stability and prosaic existence are dependent upon nonrational components of behavior. Therefore, a social-psychological theory must encompass all components and also all levels of action—including the

[47] With regard to some of this criticism, see Peter Blau and W. Richard Scott, *Formal Organizations: A Comparative Approach* (San Francisco, 1962); Alvin W. Gouldner, *Patterns of Industrial Bureaucracy* (London, 1955); Talcott Parsons, *Structure and Process in Modern Societies* (Glencoe, Ill., 1960); Howard M. Vollner and Donald Mills, eds., *Professionalization* (Englewood Cliffs, N.J., 1966).
[48] See, e.g., Norman O. Brown, *Love's Body* (New York, 1966); Philip E. Slater, *The Pursuit of Loneliness: American Culture at the Breaking Point* (Boston, 1970); Robert N. Bellah, *Beyond Belief: Essays on Religion in a Post-Traditional World* (New York, 1970).

rational, the nonrational, and the ways in which they are related.[49] Weber's work does not meet this criterion.

In this normative sociological tradition the work of Talcott Parsons is very important for us precisely because of his long-standing concern with the relationship of psychoanalytic theory to sociology and because—with the publication of *Family, Socialization, and Interaction Process*—he achieved a systematic integration of these different components and levels.[50] Parsons did this by focusing on the family as a social system of interaction in which members acquire common values or normative orientations through the processes of identification and internalization.[51]

In methodological terms Parsons faced a variety of problems which had to be resolved; certain contradictions between the essential thrusts of the two disciplines had to be reconciled before this integration could be achieved. Several related propositions in psychoanalysis had to be challenged and modified, and neither the neo-Freudians (i.e., Fromm, Horney, Sullivan) nor the cultural anthropologists writing in the late 1930s and 1940s had gone far enough, particularly in relating personality to social structure, or were critical enough of the shortcomings in their own positions.[52]

[49] We are not theoretically committed to any developmental direction. We have argued that, historically, modern society has put greater emphasis on ego orientations. Insofar as this is true, there has followed also the possibility for greater control over the external world. But this does not imply the possibility of the total elimination of the nonrational and unconscious features of socially organized behavior. In fact, in *The Wish To Be Free* we pointed out both the impossibility and the undesirability of totally conscious orientations to action. We have also indicated that the intensification of strain on individuals in modern society as a result of the emphasis on the rational control of affect can lead to reactive ideologies that stress the nonrational motives to action as a means of dealing with such strain. On this see Platt and Weinstein, "Alienation and the Problem of Social Action."

[50] Talcott Parsons and Robert F. Bales, *Family, Socialization, and Interaction Process* (Glencoe, Ill., 1955). Many of Parsons's papers on psychoanalysis and sociology are reprinted in *Social Structure and Personality*.

[51] It should be noted that Parsons's problem was one of explaining simultaneously individual development and unique features of individuality while also accounting for social order, which is both independent of, and interdependent with, individuals who participate in society. Parsons's solution relied heavily upon Durkheim's and Weber's analyses and upon two assumptions in particular: that particular groups of people share a common cultural tradition which is characterized by common values or normative orientations; and that these orientations direct personal and institutional activity. Further, it should be understood that the concept of values does not suggest the content of behavior but rather the patterns of behavior. A pattern of behavior may legitimate a wide variety of contents.

[52] There were strong areas of congruence as well, and Freud's work ultimately became very important for Parsons. See, e.g., the introduction to the paperback edition of *The Structure of Social Action*, 2 vols. (New York, 1968), 1: xi.

Parsons's modification of the classic psychoanalytic standpoint involved the following notions.

1. The fundamental psychoanalytic proposition regarding the necessarily antagonistic relationship between the individual and society was rejected. Parsons rather tended to see the interrelationship of all institutional levels in articulation with all levels of personality leading to the stabilization of social processes. Freud's notion of the development of superego and his later contributions to a theory of object relationships dominated, in Parsons's view, his idea of irreconcilable antagonism, and Parsons could maintain and then expand this position because, historically, conflict seemed to be much more a function of social change and development than that of the eruption of libidinal and aggressive contents.

In these terms Parsons argued, for example, that incest taboos are culturally rather than biologically determined, and that the structure of the erotic aspects of personality, and the patterns of personal prohibitions and sanctions, are accommodated to family and kinship networks, which are in turn related to the social patterning of such factors as mate selection, permissible objects of affection and erotic attachment, marital forms, and so forth.[53] More broadly, the family as such is functionally articulated to more general social and economic patterns. Thus, the nuclear family as it emerged in the West (physically and emotionally isolated from extended kin and other ascriptive solidarities, geographically highly mobile, differentiated by roles [especially between the parents]) is viewed as consonant with the needs of an industrial economy.[54]

2. Once Parsons understood that erotic patterns were structured by external forces, he was also able to conclude that a theory of motivation had to be in the first place not instinctual and personal (i.e., private), but subjective and social, and that all levels of personality are related to social structure and are "open" to socialization processes. It is Parsons's view, therefore, that

the distinction between instinctual and learned components of the motivational system cannot legitimately be identified with that be-

[53] See Anne Parsons, "Is the Oedipus Complex Universal? The Jones-Malinowski Debate Revisited," *Belief, Magic, and Anomie: Essays in Psychosocial Anthropology* (New York, 1969), pp. 3–66.

[54] The isolated nuclear family and the need for mobility place also a special emphasis on romantic love as the basis for mate selection and marital integration. Further, incest taboos refer only to a few immediate family members and close bilateral kin rather than to whole classes of kin structures, clans, or moities, as are often found in preliterate or non-Western societies. See, e.g., Talcott Parsons, "The Father Symbol: An Appraisal in Light of Psychoanalytic and Sociological Theory," and "The Incest Taboo in Relation to Social Structure and the Socialization of the Child," both reprinted in Parsons, *Social Structure and Personality*, pp. 34–56, 56–77.

tween the id, on the one hand, and the ego and superego on the other. Rather the categories of instinctual and learned components cut across the id, the ego, and the superego. The id, like the other sub-systems, is organized about its experiences in object relations. . . . However true it may be that advancing beyond certain early levels of development requires transcending the fixation on these early cathexes, and however much the mature personality must control them through ego and superego mechanisms, it still remains true that these are particular cases of identification and internalization of objects—not the leading example of motivation in their absence.[55]

We have already observed that by now many psychoanalysts have arrived at a similar, if not the same, position, and this requires no further comment at this point.

3. Parsons concluded further that it was necessary to explain a variety of internalized commitments above and beyond those which are acquired before and during the oedipal phase. Because social institutions are ordered and integrated on different bases than is the family, it is logically and sociologically impossible for everything that is personally acquired to be so during the first five or six years of life. For this reason it is necessary to treat social institutions as having an independent reality; it is also necessary that relationships to these institutions be treated independently of relationships to objects within the family. This viewpoint is consistent with the implications of Erikson's notion of the life cycle, and we will consider the problem again later.

As noted, we have referred to many of these points, and our indebtedness to Parsons's work should be clear. However, his contribution falls short on several counts; generally, a more detailed and empirically more viable framework is needed. That is, Parsons has suggested a general frame of reference for analysis, but he has not specified in sufficient detail the mechanisms that bind the individual to society, nor has he pursued the related problems of the variety of possible resolutions to conflict and change. The fact is, of course, that Parsons has not devoted nearly so much attention to the dynamics of change as he has to those of stability.

In relation to these objections it is also necessary to integrate theoretically an observed capacity for emotional and personal flexibility of individuals as they respond to their environment. Individuals develop the ability consciously to assess social situations in realistic terms. They can

---

[55] These thoughts on personality and social structure were expressed as early as 1951. See Parsons, "The Superego and the Theory of Social Systems," *ibid.*, pp. 17–33. The quote is from Parsons, "Social Structure and the Development of Personality: Freud's Contribution to the Integration of Psychology and Sociology," *ibid.*, p. 110.

modify commitments and alter standards that exist within a society. Given certain conditions, modification of internalized mandates is warranted and—for the sake of psychic stability—may even become necessary. Parsons has not gone far enough in this direction either. This last point is crucial, moreover, because it underscores many of the problems involved in what we mean by self-interested action, rational, irrational, and nonrational, as well as conscious and unconscious, behavior.

There is no need to consider further the shortcomings of the two socio-logical categories. We have said enough to make our point: the classic sociological problems of order and change require for adequate solution an interpretation of personality in all dimensions, and a comprehensive theoretical view must include some notion of psychic processes system-atically related to society and culture. A satisfactory formulation of such a view should include particularly psychoanalytic theories of object relationships and ego development. Object relationships must be empha-sized because it is a basic historical and sociological position to deal with events that include two or more interacting people (or classes of people), and a theory of object relationships is articulated to this level of analysis; it focuses on the problem of systematic internalized emotional relationships between and among individuals. Moreover, it is in these terms that the development of personality can be understood as determined by the cultural and social standards of particular times and places.

II. *The Sociological Implications of Psychoanalysis*

B efore we go on to elaborate the psychosocial framework discussed earlier in outline, three themes in Freud's work should be underscored. A brief consideration of these themes will provide a sense of the complexity of Freud's contribution and will help to redress the notion that Freud's singular emphasis was on biopsychological universal constants. It will also provide the background from which much of post-Freudian psychoanalysis has emerged and will serve to illuminate the sociological approach we are proposing here.

We stated earlier that Freud explained man's relationship to society, morality, and religion in terms of the resolution of oedipal conflict. But, in view of Freud's later work, this is true only in part. In fact, Freud also explained man's ties to the external world, and especially to religion, in terms of his helplessness—that is, in terms of the biologically imposed need to remain dependent upon external objects for survival for a considerable length of time. An explanation of human ties to the environment which includes such a factor as helplessness raises different questions from one which refers only to instinctual processes. Helplessness involves the control of anxiety, the mastery of stimuli, via the mediating power of adult figures.

Thus, Freud wrote that "children are protected against the dangers that threaten them from the external world by . . . their parents; they pay for this security by a fear of *loss of love* which would deliver them over helpless to the dangers of the external world." Further, Freud observed that "the child is brought up to a knowledge of his social duties by a system of loving rewards and punishments; he is taught that his security in life depends on his parents (and afterwards other people) loving him." On different occasions Freud commented on man's need to defend himself from the crushingly superior forces of nature, and on man's fear of aggression by external authority, which is "what fear of loss of love amounts to, for love is a protection against this punitive aggression."

Freud's most extensive treatment of the fear of object loss in relation to potential helplessness occurs in his work on anxiety. Freud here thought of situations of loss occurring in a developmental sequence, beginning with birth and including separation from the mother, fear of the loss of the mother's love, castration fear, and finally, fear of the superego. The mastery of this fear depends in the first place on the affect of anxiety—or, as Freud ultimately thought of it, on the adaptive and defensive capacity of "signal" anxiety. In his explanation, Freud assumed that birth was the prototypical situation of anxiety, a point at which the organism is flooded with stimuli over which it can exercise no control. However, in the maturation process, and by learning as a function of experience, this automatic, involuntary anxiety is transformed: a crucial transition occurs, from the automatic appearance of anxiety to the intentional reproduction of anxiety as a signal of danger. "Anxiety is the original reaction to helplessness in the trauma and is reproduced later on in the danger situation as a signal for help. The ego, which has undergone the trauma passively, now repeats it actively in a weakened version, hoping to have the direction in its own hands."

This process is initiated when the infant comes to recognize that objects can and do gratify needs and provide protection from internal and external dangers so that the sense of danger is displaced from the original situation at birth (an unmanageable influx of stimuli) to the condition which now realistically determines danger situations for the infant and child, loss of the object, of the object's love, and so on. At the same time, though, the child's caretaking persons support him and enable him to tolerate delay, frustration, and separation without feeling abandoned or emotionally annihilated. Thus, as the ego matures under care, it comes to assume an active role, and the individual learns to cope with loss realistically and to react with anxiety to potential situations of loss as a means of avoiding them. The ego learns to avoid excessive stimuli and to cope with moderate stimuli through adaptive activity. Anxiety reproduced as a signal of danger becomes purposeful anxiety and a part of the ego's capacity to master events.

On the one hand, then, anxiety is always linked to the original traumatic situation (birth), and any time the individual is faced with an unmanageable situation the result may be a sense of helplessness and despair. On the other hand, through maturation and experience in relation to loved objects, anxiety tends to become more remote from this condition and more consistent with reality. The gradual ability to distinguish present (actual) danger from potential danger, and situations of danger from traumatic situations, is a measure of the maturity of reality testing; failure to make such distinctions is a sign of regression.

Freud, of course, thought that most danger situations would result from instinctual pressures and that anxiety would then be reproduced as a signal leading the ego to take defensive action against the fulfillment of a wish that would prove dangerous. It is largely in this sense that Freud understood anxiety to be "reproduced as an affective state in accordance with a memory picture already present." However, Freud also understood that external events can threaten individuals too, particularly if something happens in the external world that resembles a traumatic experience of the past. These traumatic experiences are significant for the ego because they have been internalized so that some relationship between a present event and a past one is recognized—and anxiety is experienced in the same way whether an event is internal or external. The important point for us is that, while individuals may learn to avoid excessive stimuli in terms of drive manifestations, they cannot exercise the same level of control over external events.[1]

Freud, then, had two basic views of man in relation to the external world and social objects. In one view Freud assumed that man had to turn to external objects for care and protection; at the societal level this would be particularly manifest in commitments to religion, but we can readily infer the same for any institutional or collective organization. Moreover, in this context man is understood to have little tolerance for isolation and to seek social contacts; but the latter are experienced as an oppressive burden, and they also take typically a dependent form. In the second view, however, the ego's mastery of the anxiety signal allows man to cope with reality, and the internalization of parental authority into superego significantly decreases man's dependence on actual objects in the regulation of impulse or in the fulfillment of goals. Freud created believable positions in terms of both dependence and independence.

[1] The points above on object ties and fears of loss are adapted from Henri Parens and Leon J. Saul, *Dependence in Man* (New York, 1971), pp. 16–35; quotes are from pages 20–21. We have already discussed the problem of anxiety in G. M. Platt and F. Weinstein, "Alienation and the Problem of Social Action," in *The Phenomenon of Sociology*, ed. Edward Tiryakian (New York, 1971), pp. 301–10. On anxiety see also Freud, "Inhibitions, Symptoms, and Anxiety," 20: 77–174; Max Schur, "The Ego in Anxiety," in *Drives, Affects, Behavior*, vol. 1, ed. R. M. Loewenstein (New York, 1953), pp. 86–88; *idem* "The Ego and the Id in Anxiety," *Psychoanal. Stud. Child*, 13 (1958): 191, 196; George L. Engel, "Anxiety and Depression-Withdrawal: The Primary Affects of Unpleasure," *Int. J. Psychoanal.*, 43 (1962): 94; Robert W. White, *Ego and Reality in Psychoanalytic Theory*, Psychological Issues, no. 11 (New York, 1963), pp. 151–56. On Freud's shifting emphases in affect theory, see David Rapaport, "On the Psychoanalytic Theory of Affects," *Int. J. Psychoanal.*, 34 (1953): 177–98.

A second theme relates to Freud's awareness of the influence of social structure on personality—to the larger institutional organizations and not to object relations within the family, the sense in which Freud's acknowledgment of environmental influences may usually be taken. Freud wrote, for example, that the period of latency is a physiological phenomenon in man, but it gives rise "to a complete interruption of sexual life [only] in cultural organizations which have made the suppression of infantile sexuality a part of their system. This is not the case with the majority of primitive peoples." Freud observed further that "we are obliged to pay as much attention in our case histories to the purely human and social circumstances of our patients as to the somatic data and the symptoms of the disorder." In broad terms Freud related the rise of neurosis to the declining influence of religion on two occasions, and at one point, at least, he commented on the possible social and class origins of neurosis. In his last work Freud admonished his readers not to forget "to include the influence of civilization among the determinants of neurosis."[2]

We have stated that Freud did not organize a sociological position and did not see the need for one. This remains true, but, considering the way that Freud worked (that is, knowing that he was quite capable of departing from previously held positions, and that he often pulled together a seemingly random series of insights to achieve a novel synthesis), and considering too his late sociological concerns, we suggest that these thoughts should not be taken too lightly.

A third theme involves Freud's thoughts on change and development. At one point in *Totem and Taboo*, for example, Freud wrote of the "evolution of human views of the universe . . . an animistic phase followed by a religious phase, and this in turn by a scientific one." In the first phase, men ascribe omnipotence to themselves. In the second, they transfer it to the gods (although reserving to themselves the power of influencing the gods in a variety of ways). And, in the third, scientific, phase, men no

[2] The first quote on latency is from H. Hartmann, E. Kris, and R. M. Loewenstein, *Papers on Psychoanalytic Psychology*, Psychological Issues, no. 14 (New York, 1964), p. 90 (hereafter cited as *Papers*); on this see also Hans Lampl, "The Influence of Biological and Psychological Factors upon the Development of the Latency Period," in *Drives, Affects, Behavior*, vol. 1, pp. 380–87. The second quote on the social circumstances of neurosis is from Ernest Jones, *The Life and Work of Sigmund Freud*, 3 vols. (New York, 1957), 3: 336. On the relationship of the declining influence of religion to neurosis, see Kurt R. Eissler, "Death Drive, Ambivalence, and Narcissism," *Psychoanal. Stud. Child*, 26 (1971): 71; on class and neurosis, see G. Bychowski, "Psychoanalytic Reflections on the Psychiatry of the Poor," *Int. J. Psychoanal.*, 51 (1970): 503. The last quote is from Parens and Saul, *Dependence in Man*, p. 16.

longer need to ascribe omnipotence to themselves; they can abandon the illusion. Each of these phases corresponds to a stage of libidinal development and also to a stage of object relations. The animistic phase corresponds to infantile narcissism, the religious phase to the stage of object choice (of which the dominant characteristic is a child's attachment to his parents); and the scientific phase has its counterpart "in the stage at which an individual has reached maturity, has renounced the pleasure principle, adjusted himself to reality and turned to the external world for the object of his desires."[3]

However, just as Freud never pursued his ideas on the influence of culture on personality, he did not pursue this evolutionary theme, which in historical and sociological terms made more sense than the view he typically insisted upon. In terms of the theory as it existed when he wrote *Totem and Taboo*, he could not have done this adequately in any event; but he could have done it in terms of the theory as it subsequently developed. That is, in *Totem and Taboo* Freud inferred that morality, religion and social organization originated in reactions to the primal murder of the father, on the basis of clinical evidence pertaining to oepidal conflict and from the kind of anthropological work that was of interest to him. However, at the time he wrote on the subject, he was interested in id psychology and in such functions as repression and symptom formation.[4] Later Freud's interest shifted to problems of ego, an interest again based on theoretical considerations emerging from clinical evidence. The results of his work in this area, summed up particularly in *The Ego and the Id* and in *Inhibitions, Symptoms, and Anxiety*, pointed very strongly to the kind of evolutionary view briefly introduced in *Totem and Taboo*. But, though Freud changed the thrust of psychoanalytic concern from id to ego, he never applied his later conclusions in a systematic way to problems of social organization and personality development. And, though he endowed

[3] It should be understood that the narcissistic omnipotence of the so-called animistic phase is a fantasy and has no counterpart in reality. At this *ontogenetic* stage the infant is absolutely dependent upon external objects (authority) for survival itself. The infant at this stage may cathect his own needs rather than external objects, but this is a criterion of the primitive stage of development. Without the unremitting support of external persons the infant would experience overwhelming anxiety, withdrawal, and death. Freud repeated this evolutionary scheme in "The Claims of Psycho-Analysis to the Interest of the Non-Psychological Sciences," 13: 186.

[4] Heinz Hartmann, "The Ego Concept in Freud's Work," *Essays*, pp. 268–96, esp. pp. 283, 285; see also *idem*, "Comments on the Psychoanalytic Theory of the Ego," *ibid.*, p. 113. When Freud's interest shifted to the ego, he paid more attention to external influences, and then he focused, for example, on the mechanism of denial (which pertains to stimuli from external sources) as opposed to the mechanism of repression. See Arnold H. Modell, *Object Love and Reality* (New York, 1968), p. 8.

ego with significant powers in his later work,[5] he was never prepared to view man's fate in society in terms of mastery and control—or, for that matter, in terms of an ontogenetically sound sense of feared object loss and anxiety.

For example, an evolutionary view of the development of social and psychic structures could fairly be organized in terms of the problem of anxiety approximately in the way that Freud ultimately understood man's control over the affect of anxiety to develop in ontogenetic terms: that is, phase-appropriate anxiety responses evolving away from more primitive responses (automatic, rigid, violent, etc.) in the direction of greater control, in spite of internal and external pressures. The analysis of different levels of anxiety and of increased control over anxiety, which are experienced at different libidinal stages and stages of object relations, would lead logically—if projected onto social problems—to an historical investigation of the changing character of social relationships and especially of relationships to authority. Historically, it can be argued, authority has changed in terms of man's capacity to tolerate the pressure stemming from increased autonomy, personal responsibility, separation from real figures, and other such factors.[6] Considering especially the real potential that events in the external world (i.e., in the wider political and economic structures) have for disrupting internal stability, it is clear that object relations and the development of ego, or the loss of ego control and the consequent forms of regressive behavior which might follow, are just as crucial as the problems that derive from instinctual life. Such an approach corresponds generally to the scheme that Freud elaborated for the evolution of human views of the world, this itself being a factor dependent upon the mastery of anxiety and ego development.

At an earlier period in man's history, the variety of human responses to death, the unknown, darkness, and strangers, are full of magical thinking, and tend toward the creation of a world "that acknowledged no distinctions between symbol and object, a world that was created in accordance with omnipotent wishes."[7] These responses cannot be called neurotic, symptomatic, or phobic, because they are not based on regression, conflict, or displacement. Rather, these responses reflect the relative immaturity of ego and the panic-like disorientation people experienced when faced with forces in the external world which they could not

[5] See, e.g., Freud, "Inhibitions, Symptoms, and Anxiety," 20: 77–174; see also Kurt R. Eissler, *Medical Orthodoxy and the Future of Psychoanalysis* (New York, 1965), pp. 10–13.

[6] In this sense, Marx's statement that "history" presents man only with the tasks he can master can be defended.

[7] Modell, *Object Love and Reality*, pp. 16, 88.

quickly or easily master. At this level, the fundamental need was to control the danger of separation and loss. These archaic fears disappeared historically in proportion to the development of ego functions,[8] meaning, on the one hand, a decrease in projection and magical denial, and, on the other, an increase in the capacity for reality testing, delay, anticipation, secondary thought process, and so on.[9] The terms employed by Freud in *Totem and Taboo* to describe phallic oedipal conflict—the sense of guilt, remorse, renunciation—imply a degree of psychic structuralization and differentiation which quite possibly may not have existed.[10]

If one wanted to explain the origins and development of man's struggle for mastery over his environment—employing, as Freud did, ontogenetic hypotheses to shed light particularly on primitive behavior and social organization—one could very realistically, and in terms that Freud had introduced, explain this in relation to man's fear of being rendered helpless, his fear of separation and object loss, his fear of the loss of control over external reality. Thus, for example, "There is a striking parallel between the responses to a situation of helplessness, or, as we shall now say, anxiety, of Paleolithic man and the response to a situation of helplessness in the modern infant and child."[11] On the other hand, Freud understood that, in phylogenetic terms, the animistic phase he spoke of—that is, the period characterized by the pleasure principle and primary process thinking, which dominate the life of the infant up to a point and precede the reality principle and secondary process thinking—could never have been para-

---

[8] Eissler, *Medical Orthodoxy*, p. 223.

[9] See Anna Freud, *Normality and Pathology in Childhood* (New York, 1965), p. 161. Such an evolution of intellectual capacities depends upon a concomitant development of ego and superego. "First, we may expect a diminution of the tendencies toward magical thinking, as opposed to scientific thinking; of taboos and similar restrictions, frequently . . . concomitant with magical attitudes. Second, we also may expect that the ego's growing independence from the instinctual drive creates favorable conditions for solutions of problems of integration and adjustment and also influences the formation and elaboration of the superego." See also H. Hartmann, E. Kris, and R. M. Loewenstein, "Culture and Personality," *Papers*, p. 65.

[10] Margaret Mead has more recently asked, "What if Freud were right about everything except time—about which contemporary sources [i.e., the sources Freud used] were equally uninformed? What if, indeed, there had been *deeds*, not in the shadowy past of our own species, but at a much earlier period before man had developed his distinctively human growth curve with its early spurt toward apparent maturity and then the long slow plateau of latency, followed by a second spurt at adolescence?" But this even more emphatically raises the question of the degree of psychic structuralization required to experience guilt, remorse, and renunciation. See Margaret Mead, "*Totem and Taboo* Reconsidered with Respect," *Bulletin of the Menninger Clinic*, 27, no. 4 (July, 1963): 185–99, quote from 193.

[11] Modell, *Object Love and Reality*, pp. 20, 85, 88, 164. See also, e.g., Sandor Rado, "Psychodynamics of Depression from the Etiologic Point of View," in *The Meaning of Despair*, ed. W. Gaylin (New York, 1968), p. 99.

mount in early man in this way, because man could never have survived under such a condition. In psychoanalytic theory, ego functions are the guarantee of survival, and ego, therefore, must have played some significant role from the beginning. The implication, in other words, is that something more was involved originally than internal reality and the binding of erotic wishes.

The kind of evolutionary view that Freud briefly introduced, and that we suggest could have been expanded by him in terms of later theoretical summations of clinical experience, is clearly more congruent with histori-cal events than the more traditional psychoanalytic view. And, though it has never been specifically codified, reflections of it keep appearing in the psychoanalytic literature. For one thing, Freud also spoke of the history of the human race, or of the history of the Jews, in the language of "infancy" or "latency," making explicit comparisons between the develop-mental stages of individuals and groups. This also is very easily and more sensibly translated into psychic-structural terms. Thus, Freud did further comment on the evolution of superego development ("What is today an act of internal restraint was once an external one"); other psychoanalysts have taken this further in ego terms ("The adaptation to a high degree of civilization demands a greater extent in ego structuralization") and in terms of ego ideals.[12]

We can see more readily what is implied here by taking one example from the psychoanalytic literature on the development of ego ideals.

> Speaking generally, the psychic content of ego ideals can be placed into three broad, probably overlapping categories. (1) Self and object idealization can take place with respect to representation-learning made in situations in which the renunciation of instinctual drives lead[s] to such values as cleanliness, compliance, etc.; these values can be generalized into a widespread pursuit of asceticism. (2) Idealization of self and objects can occur with respect to representation-learning made in situations in which the management and regulation of instinctual drives result in ideals of control, competence, etc.; these can be generalized into a widespread pursuit of excellence. (3) Self and object idealization can take place with respect to representation-learning made in situations in which *standards of drive gratification* produce ideals

[12] On Freud's reference to society in terms of "infancy" and "latency," see W. I. Grossman and B. Simon, "Anthropomorphism," *Psychoanal. Stud. Child*, 24 (1969): 95. On Freud's comments on the evolution of superego, see Parens and Saul, *Dependence in Man*, p. 38; also on superego, see David Beres, "Psychoanalytic Notes on the History of Morality," *J. Amer. Psychoanal. Ass.*, 13 (January, 1965): 10. On the evolution of ego processes, see H. Nagera, "The Concepts of Structure and Structuralization," *Psychoanal. Stud. Child*, 22 (1967): 95.

of love, bravery, etc.; these can be generalized into a widespread pursuit of taste and sensibility.[13]

Now, each of these possibilities represents also a different degree of cathexis[14] of one of the many ego functions (e.g., control and competence require a greater cathexis of cognitive functions); and each in turn represents a higher degree of ego control over drives, as well as a more abstract, impersonal superego, more remote from actual objects. Moreover, these possibilities can be organized in a hierarchical order with regard to what is generally considered to be modern, as opposed to premodern, behavior. Thus, "ideal identifications pertaining to standards of drive gratification would appear by their very nature to predispose one much more to maintaining the actual presence of complementary ideal objects, compared to ideals of instinctual regulation and renunciation. Idealization of one's capabilities to regulate and manage instinctual drives makes, perhaps, the idealization of objects less necessary, or even less possible." Further, "medieval ideals of courtliness, taken as a whole, may be considered to represent an institutionalization of ideals of drive gratification. It is difficult to see how the industrial revolution, and all that went with it, could have taken place without an emphasis upon ideals of drive management and regulation, and perhaps even ideals of renunciation."[15]

This is not to say that an evolutionary view is the correct one, or that it is worth pursuing as opposed to other possible views. What can be said, however, is that an analysis of the development of psychic and social structures cannot be satisfactorily attempted in primarily instinctual terms, and that Freud had already put forward enough clinical and theoretical suggestions to establish this.[16] A thorough consideration of the type

[13] Irving Steingart, "On Self, Characters, and the Development of a Psychic Apparatus," *Pscyhoanal. Stud. Child*, 24 (1969): 292.

[14] "Cathexis" is one of the words invented by psychoanalysts to describe processes they have observed. It refers to "a charge of energy attached to an object." At the conscious level cathexis appears as an emotional attachment to, or feeling for, some object, and this may include the self and functions of the self. Hence we use the term in this context.

[15] Steingart, "On Self, Character, and the Development of a Psychic Apparatus," pp. 292–94. We do not necessarily accept these distinctions as accurate descriptions of historical events; we refer to this only as an example of the kind of evolutionary thought that can be organized in psychoanalytic terms. For the development and employment of evolutionary theories in contemporary sociology, see, e.g., Talcott Parsons, "Evolutionary Universals in Society," and Robert N. Bellah, "Religious Evolution," *American Sociological Review*, 29, no. 3 (June, 1964).

[16] That is, for Freud to have pursued the evolutionary theme adequately in the terms he had chosen (e.g., cognitive mastery) would have required accounting for systematic psychic-structural change in stages characterized by increasing complexity, as evidenced in enhanced ego control, more abstract, impersonal superego, and the like. Freud would have had to deal with changing psychic relations in more general terms

of evolutionary view he had introduced, in the light of later concerns and contributions, would have made this clear. In his essay on anxiety, to cite an instance, Freud observed that "the very nature of danger has a bearing upon the fact that the affect of anxiety is able to command pride of place in the mental economy." This is precisely the kind of strategic statement we refer to; it is full of implications but is never amplified.[17] Freud also pointed to the defensive functions of ego (though not to the adaptive functions of ego in the sense that Hartmann ultimately took it—i.e., that ego is partly a primary independent variable; Freud, of course, understood that in a secondary way ego functions can become relatively independent of drives). And, referring to the normative patterns of relationships that exist within a specific social structure between children and those who care for them, Freud pointed to the possibility of a developed theory of object relations. Object relations determine the pattern of, and the possibility for, behavior that is realistically oriented to the society into which an individual is born. These relationships determine also the capacity of ego to deal with conflict and anxiety which stem from external as well as internal sources, and how such ego functions as perception and cognition will develop.[18]

Such factors as these, taken together with the instinctual (libidinal and aggressive) factors, provide a sounder basis for a description of the historical past. There is pleasure in wish fulfillment, but there is also pleasure in mastery and control. And society exists as a reality inde-

---

and to account for more than one absolutely significant occasion of change in psychic organization. The focus of concern would then also have had to include such factors as anxiety stemming from the harsh conditions obtaining in the external world and the question of man's capacity to treat effectively social interaction in different realms of endeavor. And this would have been possible once the anxiety theory was revised. There would still have been serious problems, of course. We can infer from the difficulties that Freud had with the concepts of identification, internalization, introjection, and so forth, that he did not have at any point an adequate theory of object relations with which to clarify certain issues. On the difficulties with the concept of identification in Freud's work, for example, see White, *Ego and Reality in Psychoanalytic Theory*, pp. 94–124.

[17] On the basis of this statement of Freud's on anxiety, Robert White has concluded that "it can no longer be claimed that the two instinctual drives are the sole driving forces of behavior and the ultimate cause of activity. *Inhibitions, Symptoms, and Anxiety* was a revolution which destroyed forever the psychodynamic special privileges of libido and aggression." See *ibid.*, p. 156.

[18] There is no consistent theory of object relations in psychoanalysis, and the suggestions that exist have not as yet been well integrated with other aspects of theory, and certainly not so far as social and cultural problems are concerned. See, e.g., Margaret Mahler and Manuel S. Furer, *On Human Symbiosis and the Vicissitudes of Individuation*, 2 vols. (New York, 1968), vol. 1; Talcott Parsons, *Social Structure and Personality* (Glencoe, Ill., 1964), Introduction and chap. 4; Modell, *Object Love and Reality;* Erik Erikson, *Childhood and Society*, 2d ed. (New York, 1963).

pendent of the fantasies, wishes, and projections of the individuals who live within it.[19] The suggestion that man is related to society and to authority only, or even primarily, in terms of instinctual renunciation is an arbitrary one and does not adequately describe reality.[20] Broadly speaking, it can be argued that the organization and evolution of authority structures, morality, and other functions of control, reflect at least three interconnected factors. The first is man's capacity to deal realistically with large-scale tasks (i.e., the acquisition of food and shelter, the organization of defense, irrigation, etc.), and particularly those tasks which individuals and nuclear families could not cope with by themselves. The second is man's fear of separation and loss, and the anxieties that are prompted by events in the external world which threaten man with the loss of control, with ego dissolution and breakdown. The third relates to the factors of repression and sublimation of drives and impulses.

The problem, then, is to identify the causes and mechanisms of change, a problem which in terms of personality should be viewed psychoanalytically, but in a much broader way than Freud indicated. Any set of explanatory hypotheses must include a theoretical capacity to explain change historically in psychic as well as social terms. This is a problem that cannot be treated on the psychoanalytic side purely in terms of renunciation and defense, or on the historical side in terms of such generalities as the emergence or enhancement of the individual, or the development of a work ethic. The problem must be dealt with in terms of the historical development of man's internal affective, cognitive, and evaluative capacities to cope with an ever more complex environment—or the reasons for his inability to do so. At this point, explanations in these terms can best proceed in the context of psychoanalytic structural theory, though only in relation to systematic analysis at the social level—that is, in relation to a sociological theory to which the psychoanalytic standpoint is articulated.

[19] Heinz Hartmann, *Essays:* "Mutual Influences of Ego and Id," pp. 160–62; "The Theory of the Ego," pp. 120–21; "Notes on the Reality Principle," pp. 244, 248–49; "The Application of Psychoanalytic Concepts to Social Science," pp. 93, 96. "For a considerable time the reference to the instinctual demands dominated the discussions of these predispositions, and the functions of the ego were either incompletely described or the description was limited to that of mechanisms of defense at its disposal. Though at present it is generally realized that the realm of ego is wider, clinical and theoretical discussions are not conducted on the same level." H. Hartmann and E. Kris, "The Genetic Approach in Psychoanalysis," *Papers,* p. 21.

[20] This does not even describe reality in specific clinical terms. "For the child to identify with his parents' defenses becomes a way to be loved and safe from attack; it is not just a step toward renunciation." Roy Schafer, *Aspects of Internalization* (New York, 1968), p. 159.

Freud, of course, continued to view social process primarily as a reflection of internal dynamics—that is, as a matter of oedipal conflict, repression, and the "return of the repressed." With regard to varying forms of authority, such changes may be described in terms of increased consciousness—that is, of ego having conquered some territory from id processes. But at this theoretical level, as we have seen, there is, first of all, no good reason why such change should have taken place, and why it should have assumed a generalized form is not easily explained. Freud knew well that, in the context of the theory as it had developed, the return of the repressed (which necessarily he had observed only in individuals) was actually a highly idiosyncratic phenomenon. That is, Freud could not explain from individual to individual the degree of distortion which would be necessary before repressed materials could emerge into consciousness, the differences in the tenacity with which libido held to particular channels and objects, the "choice" of neurosis or when symptoms would intervene, the differential severity of superego, and so on.[21] Freud understood the implications of this at some level, as we have argued, and he tried to deal with it in *Group Psychology and the Analysis of Ego* by introducing the function of identification. At the same time, however, he never did come to any adequate conclusions on these matters, and the libidinal factors we have pointed to serve *to contradict* Freud's notion of "cultural superego" as he explained it in *Civilization and Its Discontents*.

From the standpoint of sociohistorical analysis this is the essence of the problem. A psychoanalyst examining an individual instance can determine the drive content represented in a symptom, correlate this with a psychosexual phase (oral, anal, phallic), and then say why a person has acted in a particular way. But there still remains the question of the specific choice, and, in conventional psychoanalytic terms, this must be related to the unique and idiosyncratic circumstances of an individual's life. More important, therefore, are other factors which Freud observed but never dealt with systematically at the social level of analysis. Identification is one such factor, the ego's orientations to reality, another, and so on. What these point to in the psychoanalytic context are aspects

---

[21] Thus, in his "Introductory Lectures" (15–16), Freud considered that the tenacity with which libido holds to particular channels and particular objects is "an independent factor varying in individuals, the determining conditions of which are completely unknown to us." Much later Freud wrote again ("Analysis Terminable and Interminable," 23) about individuals who display a peculiar "adhesiveness of libido." "The processes which their analysis sets in motion are so much slower than in other people because they apparently cannot . . . detach libidinal cathexis from one object and displace it to another, although we can find no particular reason for this cathectic fidelity."

of behavior which "are not clearly traceable to the content of the original drive or the earlier drive conflict. Thus, whereas it is possible to see reaction-formation against anal-erotic impulses in the compulsive's hand-washing or overconcern with cleanliness, the reliance on reaction-formation itself (in contrast, for example, with reliance on the mechanism of repression), the moralistic attitudes, and the intensity of activity and work that are usually associated with such symptoms are not easily derived from the specific content of the drive conflict."[22] In short, sociological factors influence personality, and these too must be made explicit.

One of the problems in this connection which existed in Freud's day and which still exists is that no element or aspect of psychoanalytic theory can match the organizing power of libido theory, with its well-known specific phases, fixation points, and regressive contents—all of which have been well described in the literature (especially by Freud) and are evident enough. Not even psychoanalytic explanations of aggression, the other instinctual component, come close to the sophistication of libido theory—let alone problems of ego and object relations. The theory of symptom formation, for example, which obviously must include the factors of aggression, ego development, and object relations, is still most cogently presented in terms of the libido theory. For this reason, what we often see in the applications of psychoanalysis to history, and especially in relation to the analysis of groups and societies, is an attempt to deal with these complex problems by analogy with the patterns of libidinal frustration and symptom formation in the individual.[23] And hence we have the language of father-son conflict and of psychosexual resolutions to conflict in oral, anal, or phallic terms.

Freud obviously did this, and not only in libido terms, about which he knew a great deal, but also in terms of aggression, about which he knew much less. In *Civilization and Its Discontents*, which has often served as the theoretical basis for historical and cultural analysis, Freud dealt

[22] David Shapiro, *Neurotic Styles* (New York, 1965), p. 5. Shapiro concludes that "Freud was aware of the insufficiency of an attempt to solve the problem of symptom choice exclusively on the basis of libidinal development, conflict, and fixation." However, Freud never integrated the other aspects of the problem, ego development, object relationships, etc. On the aspect of ego psychology pertaining to motives and aims not directly linked to sexual origins, and the theoretical problems involved, see George S. Klein, "The Ego in Psychoanalysis," *Psychoanal. Rev.*, 56, no. 4 (1969–70): 511–25.

[23] Martin H. Stein, "The Problem of Character Theory," *J. Amer. Psychoanal. Ass.*, 17, no. 3 (July ,1969): 693. Moreover, there still is not a complete theory in psychoanalysis on how individual character becomes what it is, much less on how to account for the similarity of features in a population. This will require a series of sociological hypotheses. See *ibid.*, p. 697.

with aggression as an instinctual problem independent of sexuality and with its role in the evolution of civilization. On the basis of the repression, sublimation, or displacement of aggression, Freud tried to explain the binding power of society, particularly in terms of superego (internalized morality) and guilt.

In this work, for example, Freud ascribed the difficulty of cultural development to "the inertia of the libido, to its disinclination to give up an old position for a new one." But both earlier and later he indicated that this tenacity of libido, or adhesiveness of libido, is an independent factor that varies in individuals, and he did not know why. Thus, on what basis was it possible to generalize this libidinal factor for a population? Freud wrote also that, as long as things go well with a man, his conscience is tolerant, but when things go wrong his conscience becomes harsh and punitive—and Freud observed that "whole peoples have behaved in this way, and still do." But, if the severity of conscience depends as much upon the child's fantasies as it does upon what the parents do, on what basis was this generalization made? In order to resolve the contradiction here, Freud immediately added that the individual is not all that independent of his environment, and, then, in order to confirm and bolster his conclusion, he moved over to the phylogenetic explanation: "We cannot get away from the assumption that man's sense of guilt springs from the Oedipus complex and was acquired at the killing of the father by the brothers banded together."[24]

Now Freud understood the scientific criterion of parsimony as well as anyone. Why did he use two hypotheses when one would do? Actually, Freud was not conceding very much to the power of the environment, and, in fact, his suggestion does not make much sense without a corresponding theory of ego and of object relations. Freud's reference to the environment as a determinative factor is important as a legitimation for work that was done after him, but, in *his* work, environment was not intended to explain as much as the phylogenetic hypothesis. As no one is going to defend the phylogenetic view at this point, for all intents and purposes we are back where we started: idiosyncratic factors were used to describe generalized social behavior.

It is necessary to conclude, therefore, that it is not possible to render an analysis of historical and cultural problems in terms of drives and psychosexual phases. In particular it is not possible to generate a model for political behavior (to take the inevitable example) from the classic description of oedipal conflict. At the very least it must be noted that

[24] Freud, "Civilization and Its Discontents," 21: 108, 126, 130–31.

the oedipal situation may be universal in the sense that each individual in early life experiences intense conflict at this developmental point, and learns basic social moralities and to distinguish himself from others in sexual and other terms. But the analysis of oedipal situations must be adjusted to the varieties of social life as these have been described in the anthropological and historical literature.[25] The oedipal drama does not have to take the same form everywhere, nor is the oedipal conflict the only decisive conflict in the life of the individual, nor does change within a particular institution or society have to have oedipal implications, nor does the oedipal situation have to be the most crucial period of individual growth in a systematic social sense.

There are too many weaknesses in Freud's analysis of the bases upon which society is organized. Freud used the oedipal frame of reference on the assumption that social organization is a reflection of internal conflict and its resolution in the family, and that the types of conflict which occur within the individual because of life in the family will be displaced onto the wider world. He assumed further that social structure exists primarily to keep erotic and aggressive wishes under control in terms of guilt and renunciation. Thus, he never had to give up his basic views on the question of men in society: "The whole course of the history of civilization is no more than an account of the various methods adopted by mankind for 'binding' their unsatisfied wishes."[26]

[25] Anne Parsons, "Is the Oedipus Complex Universal? The Jones-Malinowski Debate Revisited," *Belief, Magic, and Anomie: Essays in Psychosocial Anthropology* (New York, 1969), pp. 3–66; Hartmann, Kris, and Loewenstein, "Culture and Personality," *Papers*, pp. 98–99.

[26] Freud, "The Claims of Psycho-Analysis to the Interest of the Non-Psychological Sciences," 13: 186. Freud, for example, dealt with superego in *Civilization and Its Discontents* solely in terms of its punitive functions. This is another instance of Freud's having already arrived in clinical terms at a more complex and differentiated view than was made evident in this work on man in society. What Roy Schafer has called "the loving and beloved superego" does not appear in this work, although Schafer traced this concept back to other of Freud's writings. By way of explanation, Schafer writes that "normal courage, endurance, and ability to withstand intense stimulation or deprivation, all depend on the feeling of being recognized and attended to by the superego or destiny. This is another place where a major theoretical position [was] implied [in Freud] but not worked out. What we ordinarily call ego strength, for example, is seen in this connection as a matter of the mutual relations of ego and superego; the availability, and possibly the quantity, of energies in the ego to be used in adaptation seem to depend in large part on a *faithful, benevolent superego*." Roy Schafer, "The Loving and Beloved Superego in Freud's Structural Theory," *Psychoanal. Stud. Child*, 15 (1960): 175; italics added. See also p. 170 for Schafer's explanation of why Freud stressed the punitive aspects of superego.

On the one hand, then, the kind of analysis which Freud attempted requires additional theoretical bases; on the other hand, it is quite possible that those behaviors which must be described in libidinal and energy terms as idiosyncratic, as well as those behaviors which cannot be traced back to the original drive conflict, are affected by social-structural factors. The additional theoretical factors (ego development and object relations, based now on evidence derived from more recent work done on border-line, narcissistic, and schizophrenic disorders, and on more recent at-tempts to deal with internalization and identification)[27] have been orga-nized to a degree and somewhat integrated with regard to problems of adult and childhood experience. But the process of integration has not proceeded nearly fast enough with regard to social-historical investigation. Thus, when historians have employed psychoanalytic concepts at this level, too often they have ended up writing clinical case studies (as op-posed to history), or they have tried to make historically adequate generalizations based on inferences from psychoanalytic hypotheses and assumptions that could not support such generalizations.[28]

---

[27] As Anna Freud, Hartmann, and others have observed, the term "infantile neurosis" is overworked because a lot of what goes on does not come under the heading of neurosis, either because it is not the result of conflict at all, or because it is not the result of the kind of internal conflict where danger comes to a head in the oedipal phase. Disturb-ances can derive from excessive delay in the oganization of vital ego functions, or from primary disturbances of narcissism, or from inadequate object relations (leading to a lack of ego control, faulty superego, to a combination of both), and so on. While some of these problems are related to constitutional factors, primarily they are related to the kind of environment the child finds, the kinds of demands that are made on him, and the way that important figures facilitate or hamper ego and superego develop-ment. See Anna Freud, "Links between Hartmann's Ego Psychology and the Child Analyst's Thinking," in *Psychoanalysis: A General Psychology*, ed. R. M. Loewenstein *et al.* (New York, 1966), p. 23. On identification and internalization see p. 25, n. 42, of the present volume.

[28] We can take the effort of one historian as an example. Rudolph Binion, in his psychoanalytic study of Lou Andreas Salome, discounted the effects of society on the individual in these terms: "I can go no farther—if even this far—toward validating the common claim that background shapes the mind and character. . . . *Perhaps she might as well have been a Basque peasant's or Welsh fisherman's daughter for all the real difference it would have made to her mentality and personality. Her father was higher and mightier than most, but he need not have been for her father romance to have had the same outcome: witness Jesus* [italics added]." One can quickly see that differences in time, place, and social back-ground do not matter (which eliminates history). At the same time, the details of the biography, the specific resolution of the conflict engendered by the father romance, viewed from the psychosexual standpoint, are so idiosyncratic that no generalization about society could possibly be made (which eliminates sociology). R. Binion, *Frau Lou: Nietzsche's Wayward Disciple* (Princeton, 1968), p. 31. For an example of the other error—that is, predicating generalizations on idiosyncratic features of analysis—see Arthur Mitzman's biography of Max Weber, *The Iron Cage* (New York, 1970).

This is the result, in part, of Freud's emphasis on internal as opposed to external reality,[29] of continued reliance upon Freud's work exclusively, or of a misapprehension of what post-Freudian writers such as Erikson are about. But, since Freud himself had already perceived the shortcomings inherent in the classic approach—as evidenced in the appearance of the structural theory (1923), the revised theory of anxiety (1926), and his observations on the preoedipal mother (1931)[30]—in the most general terms this is a result of the failure to think through the implications of the problems presented by such concepts as identification and internalization, and by the long-term effects of the environment. Psychoanalysts, at any rate, have been forced to contend with these factors, and this is the reason for, and the basis upon which, the psychoanalytic ego psychology and at least some theories of object relationships were developed.

Primarily what changed was the attitude toward ego—that is, toward man's capacity to bring the world under control and make relatively conscious choices with regard to a variety of social experiences. In *The Ego and the Id* (1923), Freud viewed the ego as "a man on horseback, who has to hold in check the superior strength of the horse [i.e., id processes]." While this passage is typically taken as an example of Freud's deference to the determinative power of the id, it must also be observed that ego can control these processes, and this too requires analysis. Moreover, in the later *Inhibitions, Symptoms, and Anxiety* (1926), the ego appears in an even stronger position against the id. The ego exerts great power over drives by means of repression, and "the reader can hardly finish Freud's 1926

[29] One recurrent explanation of this emphasis is that when Freud discovered early in his psychoanalytic work that the seductions and traumatic experiences reported to him by his patients were fantasy wishes and not actual external events, he tended to de-emphasize the external world, and he underestimated reality experiences thereafter. Whatever the case, it was not until the late 1930s that Freud's students began to shift this emphasis in a systematic way, and only at that point did there emerge "an ever increasing readiness to pay more attention to external reality as a source of variability in ego development, on the one hand, and on the other, to the ego itself, or many of its functions, as an instrument of adaptation *to* external reality in a broader sense than had hitherto been considered." See John D. Benjamin, "Discussion of Hartmann's *Ego Psychology and the Problem of Adaptation*," in *Psychoanalysis*, ed. Loewenstein *et al.*, p. 35. See also Ernst Kris, "Development and Problems of Child Psychology," *Psychoanal. Stud. Child*, 5 (1950): 26; W. Barrett and D. Yankelovich, *Ego and Instinct: Psychoanalysis and the Science of Man*, ed. Alice Mayhew (New York, 1970), p. 33.

[30] Psychoanalysts are themselves quite capable of resistance, especially to innovation, as witness this statement by Ruth Mack Brunswick: "When we attempt to examine the origins and precursors of the oedipus complex, we encounter among analysts an opposition not unlike the earlier opposition of the outside world to the oedipus complex itself. The use of the term 'preoedipal sexuality' seems to arouse a certain loyalty to the oedipus complex as if its validity were being threatened." R. M. Brunswick, "The Preoedipal Phase of Libido Development," *Psychoanal. Quart.*, 9 (1940): 293–94.

treatise on anxiety without getting the impression that the ego, once endowed with the efficacy of the anxiety signal, is strong and well prepared to navigate the treacherous waters, with their dangerous undercurrents and backflows." Later still, Freud spoke of the "taming" of drives, or the mastery of drives, "through the mental representative of the instinct becoming subordinated to a larger organization, and finding its place in a coherent unity." Instinct is "brought into harmony with the ego, no longer seeking for independent satisfaction." These last statements imply a very high order of ego control, higher than that implied in the earlier statements on the ego, and perhaps higher than many psychoanalysts would concede. Moreover, Freud did not always hold to these views on ego, and he would sometimes also stress the ego's weaknesses.[31] But, regardless of arguments over degree, the pattern was set; the ego became the center of concern, and essentially two directions were pursued—one by Hartmann, Kris, Anna Freud, and others in the direction of ego development and object relationships, including particularly Hartmann's theoretical statements on autonomous ego functions (or, to be more explicit, on the "relatively autonomous characteristics of certain ego functions"); and one by Erikson in the direction of the effects of social structure on personality.[32]

[31] Barrett and Yankelovich, *Ego and Instinct*, p. 10; see also Eissler, *Medical Orthodoxy*, pp. 9–14.

[32] Many problems of ego development were clarified in particular by the systematic amplification of the role of the mother in the preoedipal period, and this too made emphasis on the external world inevitable. See Kris, "Development and Problems of Child Psychology," *passim*. Further, what Hartmann meant by autonomous ego functions again is that, biologically speaking, some ego functions are independent of the instinctual drives, while others become independent of their instinctual origins in a secondary way—i.e., ego functions have a primary and a secondary autonomy. The division of labor among Hartmann, Kris, Anna Freud, and Erikson is not a hard and fast one. The contributions of all these authors overlap; Hartmann, for example, certainly stressed the social dimension in relation to psychoanalytic theory. On the relation of Hartmann's work to Erikson's (and of the relation of both to Freud and to the main body of theory) see David Rapaport's introduction to Erik Erikson's *Identity and the Life Cycle*, Psychological Issues, no. 1 (New York, 1959), pp. 12–16. See also Barrett and Yankelovich, *Ego and Instinct*, pp. 95–154; and Grossman and Simon, "Anthropomorphism," pp. 98–99. Heinz Hartmann is not very well known outside psychoanalytic circles, and he certainly does not have the reputation that a number of other writers in this tradition can boast. But our reliance on Hartmann's work in so many respects in this chapter should indicate the breadth and importance of his contributions to psychoanalytic theory. "It was Heinz Hartmann, whom many believe to be the main architect of the post-Freudian period, who launched the program for enlarging the scope of psychoanalysis beyond the unconscious and the neurotic." Barrett and Yankelovich, *Ego and Instinct*, p. 96. The specific quote on ego autonomy is from a review of *Ego and Instinct* by Leopold Bellak; see *Psychoanal. Rev.*, 40, no. 2 (1971): 358.

It should be understood that this shift in emphasis, which, by establishing an adequate basis for explaining autonomous as well as regressive psychic functions enabled psychoanalysis to become a general psychology, was the result of substantial clinical and theoretical observation.[33] The criticism has been raised that this was intended—or ultimately served only—to domesticate the discipline.[34] But this is an irrelevant factor. Freud had wanted to know how the ego survives in various conflicts, which are always present, without falling ill.[35] And psychoanalysts were able to observe in their daily experience that people who could not function effectively were enabled to do so by therapy, and people who were in therapy for whatever reasons were still capable of handling various aspects of their lives in fairly responsible ways. Such people were even capable of making important decisions for themselves and others without collapsing from the effort. That the ego could function under stress had to be accounted for theoretically in a systematic way.[36]

This concern led to a conceptual emphasis on the ability of men to observe and attend to the problems they are faced with in a realistic, as opposed to a wishful, way. Behavior may be emotionally founded, but (relatively speaking, of course) decisions can be free of regressive pulls and free of hampering distortions. Psychoanalytic theory moved away from the notion of the helpless and beleaguered ego, caught on three sides by id, superego, and unrelenting reality, waging therefore a constant defensive struggle. Freud initially pointed the way in various writings, and one can fairly assume that he understood that this was bound to happen to a much greater extent, although he was not the one primarily responsible for it. Robert Waelder reports that once, in response to a discussion on a multidimensional system of characterology, Freud said

[33] On one level, for example, the guarantee of man's survival rests with the ego, and this had to be explained theoretically; on another level this ego-psychological standpoint derives from the need to explain psychoses and other forms of regression to early ego states.

[34] See, e.g., G. W. Domhoff, "Two Luthers," *Psychoanal. Rev.*, 57, no. 1 (1970): 5–17.

[35] Freud, "Neurosis and Psychosis," 19: 152, 150.

[36] For example, "We hear him [i.e., the patient] describe his efficient and successful activities in a highly complex business or profession, while he behaves with us so often as if he were passive, helpless, and childlike." Stein, "The Problem of Character Theory," p. 695. It should also be noted, then, that the clinical situation, as opposed to the historian's situation, does not always and inevitably favor the clinician. The latter rarely sees as much of a person as a whole as the historian does, and he rarely sees the subject functioning ably in different contexts. Analytic observation is weighted in favor of the archaic; behavior is subject to considerable distortion resulting from regressions provoked by the analysis itself. *Ibid.* See also Richard Siegal, "What are Defense Mechanisms?" *J. Amer. Psychoanal. Ass.*, 17, no. 3 (July, 1969): 787; and Phyllis Greenacre, *The Quest for the Father* (New York, 1963), pp. 10–11.

that he felt "like the skipper of a barge who had always hugged the coast, who now learned that others, more adventurous, had set out for the open sea. He wished them well, but he could no longer participate in their endeavor."[37]

This concern also led to a conceptual emphasis on the empirical and theoretical involvement of social-structural factors in personality development. Ego in these terms was then understood to develop not only on the basis of drive and defense but also and especially on the basis of identification and internalization. This was the implication—to cite an instance—of Anna Freud's observation of the infant ego's hostility to the drives based on identification with the nurturant mother, an observation which led easily to the further proposition that endogenous potentialities are structured by specific cultural patterns.[38] This approach tied the individual to the values and mandates of specific times and places, and for the first time a basis was provided within psychoanalytic theory for systematic statements about behavior predicated upon connections between psychic and social structure. One could now begin to get around the problem raised by the emphasis on drive, and especially libido, theory, by the idiosyncratic content of psychosexual conflicts, and the like. It was on the basis of such factors as these that both Hartmann and Erikson some time ago indicated that a sociological orientation is necessary for psychoanalytic theory.

However, this raises some serious questions with regard to the basic thrust of psychoanalysis, and with regard to the view that Freud had of his discipline. Once the sociological dimension is introduced, different kinds of questions have to be asked, questions that relate to theory and therapy, but also to the study of the historical past. For example, in *Group Psychology and the Analysis of the Ego*, which we spoke about briefly above, Freud still thought "of a type of behavior that is not limited to definite epochs of history, but that under certain conditions will repeat itself, . . . over and over again in the history of mankind, with essential elements remaining unchanged."[39] However, from a social-historical point of view it is necessary to think of specific social structures at given times, and the unconscious and conscious contents and mechanisms must be interrelated with the institutional and cultural organizations, and with the values and norms that structure activity in specific instances.

---

[37] R. Waelder, opening remarks to the panel discussion "Neurotic Ego Distortion," *Int. J. Psychoanal.*, 39 (1958): 243–44.

[38] See, e.g., Freud, "An Outline of Psychoanalysis," 23: 201.

[39] Heinz Hartmann, "On Rational and Irrational Action," *Essays*, p. 51.

In other words, there may be, in psychoanalytic terms, an identical functioning of such basic factors as the pleasure and reality principles, an identity of primary instinctual needs, and an approximate identity of some defense mechanisms (regression, repression, projection). But, "as to the structure of the superego, the individual defense mechanisms, the extent of identification, the distance or closeness of the superego, the sense of identity, and a long list of other factors—with regard to all these, there is no reason to assume an identity through all historical periods."[40] That is, political authority, forms of economic practice and religious doctrine, levels of autonomous behavior, attachments to morality, and a variety of other social activities are different from one time and place to another. But, granting that, how can the differences be accounted for? More particularly, what kind of hypotheses are necessary in order to integrate and explain the greatest quantity of data? If (as Hartmann, for one wrote) social reality is an independent factor, if society is not merely a projection of unconscious fantasies and wishes, not merely a reproduction of familial relationships, and if the kinds of historical change we have described actually occurred, it is necessary to postulate that changes in social structure systematically produce changes in psychic structure.[41] Classical psychoanalytic theory always viewed the problem the other way around, but it is hard to see, for historical and sociological analysis at any rate, how this position can be maintained.

There are certain problems in psychoanalytic work in which this relationship between social and psychic structure is rather easy to identify, and an example of such a problem will illuminate the approach we have just outlined. Take, for instance, the following statement from the recent psychoanalytic literature: "The sense-of-self, its conservation and range of reversible identifications, *is now for the adolescent, in principle, limitless*. This significant new kind of identification for the adolescent—that any and all identification constitutes only *a personal decision and creative tool about meaning* —ought not to be mistaken for the familiar comparison between fantasy

[40] Eissler, *Medical Orthodoxy*, pp. 153–54; Hartmann, Kris, and Loewenstein, "Culture and Personality," *Papers*, p. 109.

[41] "Society is not a projection of unconscious fantasies, though it offers many possibilities for such projection and their study reveals to us the influence of unconscious factors on men's attitudes to society." "Institutions that characterize a social system have often been interpreted solely as the direct expression of the unconscious and conscious desires of people living in that system, as if reality were no more than a wish-fulfillment. This approach avoids the problem raised by my statement that social structures are, in the first place, imposed upon the growing individual as an external reality." Hartmann, "The Application of Psychoanalytic Concepts to Social Science," *Essays*, pp. 93–96.

and reality."[42] This kind of psychoanalytic suggestion can be fully appreciated only in the light of historical and sociological perspectives. This statement refers to the organization of self-images and to behaviors which are, historically speaking, only very recent occurrences. Further, it refers only to a highly industrialized and pluralized society where multiple roles are acceptable and obligatory, and where the choices are open-ended. This statement is also indicative of the fact that society has had to systematically organize—or impose—tasks in this maturational period (which is characterized in any event by great conflict) of a rather novel sort. In general this must be seen as the result of the development of industrialization and democratization processes that are affecting familial and educational processes in novel ways. Changes at the level of social structure, therefore, have prompted systematic changes at the psychic level. This kind of statement appears in the psychoanalytic literature because analysts are encountering the problems raised by the increased levels of autonomy in the therapeutic situation.

There is no conflict between basic psychoanalytic assumptions with regard to instinctual life, the unconscious, repression, and the like, and this kind of sociopsychological statement. There are different levels of abstraction at which it is permissible to view the same data for different purposes. At a point in one of his essays, discussing the interpretation of a dream, Erikson stated that, "in the context of one interpretation, the dream image would be primarily symbolic of a sexual idea which is to be warded off, in the second a representation of a danger to the continuous existence of individual identity (and thus of the 'ego')."[43] Both points of view are "right," and there is no contradiction between the two. This position may be stated in broader terms, as in the following example: "Variations in the level of abstraction are evident if one considers the formulations of Abraham, Freud, and Parsons. Abraham discusses [for example] identification in terms of organ language: the breast or the penis

---

[42] Steingart, "On Self, Character, and the Development of a Psychic Apparatus," p. 296. "A self concept now exists formally for an adolescent as something that is an entity unto itself—*and hence is man made*—not as something somehow embedded and given in the very concrete flux of his experience." (The italics in this quote are in the original; those in the quote in the text were added.) On the relationship between social structure and adolescence, see also E. Pumpian-Mindlin, "Vicissitudes of Infantile Omnipotence," *Psychoanal. Stud. Child*, 24 (1969): 221–22; Z. Alexander Aarons, "Normality and Abnormality in Adolescence," *ibid.*, 25 (1970): 309–10; and Joseph Barnett, "Dependency Conflicts in the Young Adult," *Psychoanal. Rev.*, 58, no. 1 (1971): 114. It seems to us that the problems of adolescence in this society at this time have really made an impression which impels an observer to find, to some extent, causal factors in the external world. On this issue, see, e.g., Ruth Benedict, "Continuities and Discontinuities in Cultural Conditioning," *Psychiatry*, 1 (1938).

[43] Erik Erikson, "The Nature of Clinical Evidence," *Daedalus*, 87 (Fall, 1958): 82.

is eaten up and identified with, etc. . . . [Referring to an example he had cited earlier, the author says that] Freud discusses identification in terms of interpersonal conflict. . . . Parsons discusses identification in terms of societal needs and processes: the boy is brought up to renounce his early tie to his mother and his succeeding tie to his family unit, and to move out into the wider community, etc. These are not mutually antagonistic formulations."[44]

However, while it is true that there is no fundamental logical conflict among these different ways of looking at the same problem, it is also true that there are some basic analytic incongruities. For example, Freud pointed to the influence of the external world while Abraham did not; Parsons's view, however, most readily permits the integration of personal, social, and historical data. From the standpoints of Abraham and Freud, there is no way to explain why identification processes have changed or continue to change with changing social and cultural circumstances. It is particularly clear in Abraham's case that psychic structure operates according to its own autonomous laws, and questions of where and when really do not matter.

Thus, there is a sociological side to psychoanalytic problems, and certain problems are better understood from a sociological point of view. However, as far as the application of psychoanalytic theory to history is concerned, except in the work of Erikson and his students, the sociological dimension has rather resolutely been ignored. Erikson is quite right when he states that "the phenomenon and the concept of *social organization*, and its bearing on the individual ego was . . . for the longest time, shunted off by patronizing tributes to the existence of 'social factors.' "[45] The most

---

[44] Schafer, *Aspects of Internalization*, pp. 168, 165. For example, it would be a consistent psychoanalytic position to assume that "morality also develops endogenously in some respects—it is not all acquired by identification." Such a standpoint has its uses in the explanation of the idiosyncratic features of particular personalities, but from a systematic sociological point of view it is not a necessary hypothesis. Roy Schafer, "Ideals, Ego Ideal, and Ideal Self," in *Motives and Thought: Essays in Honor of David Rapaport*, ed. R. R. Holt, Psychological Issues, no. 18/19 (New York, 1967), p. 143.

[45] Erikson, *Identity and the Life Cycle*, p. 19. Involved in this issue too is the dispute between the "orthodox" psychoanalysts and the "neo-Freudians"—particularly Horney, Fromm, and Sullivan. These writers also approached problems from the social side, but in so doing they eliminated important psychoanalytic hypotheses. This allowed the psychoanalysts to speak of "sociologism" while continuing to practice a psychoanalytic reductionism. The difference between Erikson's approach and the so-called cultural approach has been summarized by Rapaport in the following terms: "The crucial characteristic of this [Erikson's] psychosocial theory of ego development, and of Hartmann's adaptation theory (in contrast to the 'culturalist' theories) is that they offer a conceptual explanation of the individual's social development by tracing the unfolding *of the genetically social character of the human individual* in the course of his encounters with the social environment at each phase of his epigenesis. Thus it is not

serious effect of this has been that, while social change obviously occurs and must be accounted for, no sound theory of change has ever emerged from psychoanalytic thought.[46]

Among psychoanalysts, Erikson has gone the farthest with psychoanalytic explanations in social terms. Relating his work to Freud's psychosexual standpoint, and complementing the post-Freudian developments in ego psychology, Erikson has contributed to a sociological approach to psychoanalytic theory in three ways. First, he has indicated the positive as well as the negative consequences of the resolutions of conflict attached

---

assumed that societal norms are grafted upon the genetically social individual by 'disciplines' and 'socialization,' but that the society into which the individual is born makes him its member by influencing *the manner in which* he solves the tasks posed by each phase of his epigenetic development." Rapaport's introduction to Erikson's *Identity and the Life Cycle*, p. 15. On the "neo-Freudians," see J. A. C. Brown, *Freud and the Post-Freudians* (New York, 1963), pp. 129–89.

[46] The fact is that the psychoanalytic literature that historians tend to learn from or to borrow from (primarily Freud himself) does not take seriously enough the world beyond the individual and the family. By and large, then, statements on cultural and historical phenomena still stress instinctual factors and especially the psychosexual ramifications of oedipal conflict. As we noted, Freud himself was rather convinced of the phylogenetic roots of the problem—that is, of the "inheritance of acquired characteristics, which would account for phenomena such as the (ubiquitous) occurrence of sexual symbols and . . . the occurrence of oedipal conflict." Thus Freud insisted that the intensity of castration fears that he saw in male children could not be accounted for in terms of actual threats experienced in the phallic phase; only the memory of the race could satisfactorily explain that intensity. Hartmann, Kris, and Loewenstein, "Culture and Personality," *Papers*, p. 96; Hartmann and Kris, "The Genetic Approach in Psychoanalysis," *ibid.*, p. 18. On Freud's phylogenetic hypotheses, see also, e.g., Derek Freeman, "Totem and Taboo: A Reappraisal," in *Man and His Culture: Psychoanalytic Anthropology after "Totem and Taboo,"* ed. W. Muensterberger (London, 1969).

On the one hand, as we have noted, psychoanalysts would not attempt seriously to defend these phylogenetic assumptions, and, on the other hand, a good deal of work since Freud testifies to the effects of pre- and postoedipal factors on relations to the external world. "In the case history of Little Hans a few data on the personality of the parents are given, particularly on the personality of the mother who had been Freud's patient. If the same case history were reported today, this problem would undoubtedly be given considerable prominence. This difference is due not only to an increase in observational data but clearly reflects a change in theoretical assumptions; i.e., the importance of environmental factors on earliest stages of development in general and the role of preoedipal experiences specifically." H. Hartmann, E. Kris, and R. M. Loewenstein, "The Function of Theory in Psychoanalysis," *Papers*, p. 119. But, in addition to this, because the only environmental factors that Freud dealt with regularly were the father, the mother, and the parents (taken as a unit), and because the individual (as derived from a family situation) was understood to be the essential social factor, it is difficult in the context of Freud's work to judge action as realistic, independent of instinctual origins, or relatively or potentially so. Political behavior, as we have said, is forever being interpreted as a repetition of father and son conflict. Freud had no sociological standpoint, nor was he interested in organizing it. In these terms, it does not help for psychoanalysts to continue to insist that "psychoanalysis is Freud." (See, e.g., Eissler, *Medical Orthodoxy*, p. 202.)

to the several developmental stages; by indicating the sources of strength involved in human endeavor Erikson helped to correct the earlier picture that one might easily have come away with—namely, that anything a man did that was significant enough to be worthy of attention must have had some neurotic core. Second, Erikson elaborated psychosocial stages of development which complement the psychosexual stages described by Freud; this is precisely the kind of step which links the demands made upon children and adults to the specific society in which they live. And, third, Erikson extended developmental stages beyond the oedipal and latency periods through adolescence to maturity and old age.[47]

Thus, Erikson took a crucial step in a sociological direction: in brief, "ego strength develops from an interplay of personal and social structure." Ernst Kris wrote some twenty years ago that psychoanalytic child psychology had shifted toward an "environmentalist" position, while Hartmann said as much for ego psychology in general. But it was Erikson who showed how behavioral modalities are affected in earlier *and later* years by the particular requirements of social structures. However, once Erikson demonstrated the usefulness and the necessity of distinguishing developmental stages throughout life, it also became necessary to develop a sociological position with regard to the institutions beyond the family which affect behavior in the more mature years. Erikson's position, therefore, leads back to the conclusion we arrived at earlier: social-structural factors will affect events at the psychic level. That is, once the position is taken that social reality exists independently of projection and wish

---

[47] The eight stages are: Basic trust versus mistrust; autonomy versus shame and doubt; initiative versus guilt; industry versus inferiority; identity versus identity diffusion; intimacy versus isolation; generativity versus stagnation; integrity versus despair. It should perhaps be noted that these stages which Erikson has developed are as dependent upon sociological factors as they are upon psychological factors. That is, psychoanalysis as a codified discipline has itself developed out of conditions derived from the industrialization process. However, if we could imagine a preindustrial psychoanalyst describing the stages of man's life, autonomy, initiative, and industry would not be the words applied to them, and the ideal resolutions of conflict in each stage would have been quite different. Further, there might have been some trouble with the number of stages in psychosocial terms, age-graded in the way they are. That is, puberty might have been discussed, while adolescence might not. Erikson's concepts imply a particular kind of highly pluralized social structure to which individuals are socialized. What need was there, for example, for socialized initiative in relatively static and hierarchical societies that were organized around ascriptive criteria of class, race, and blood, and that stressed passive acceptance of social situations rather than insist upon man's capacity to change his circumstances? Erikson's concept of identity must be viewed in the same terms. Perhaps identity has always been a problem, but, as with adolescence, the special circumstances of our own period—the kinds of pressures put on young adults for choices, control, etc.—make identity formation a particularly critical period. See, e.g., Benedict, "Continuities and Discontinuities in Cultural Conditioning."

fulfillment; that people are born into specific social structures with figures, symbols, and institutions that are not merely symbolic representations of original familial objects; that stages all through life will be the source of conflict and of new resolutions (either in autonomous or regressive terms); and that people adapt to, or are in conflict with, these institutions at their own level, it becomes necessary also to concede the primary and original way that society can affect the individual—and to deal with object relations, internalization, identification, loss, anxiety, and so on, in these terms.

In this way Erikson's social perspective adds a necessary dimension to psychoanalytic thought. Logically and empirically speaking, people do eventually become affectively attached to different institutions beyond the family. Moreover, it is reasonable to suppose that, if society did not provide, through the family, some systematic means of becoming attached to other, larger units, no social tasks could be accomplished. The erotic ties that bind the family together predispose any individual to remain within it. Further, this need to direct activity outside the family unit should not be viewed merely as defensive, a function of repression and sublimation which serves to keep oedipal (or preoedipal) aggression under control. There are positive functions of mastery over the environment which are facilitated by withdrawal from the familial matrix, and there are tasks which can be fulfilled only on a higher social level. There is, particularly in the modern world, no inevitable identity between family and society; and, even in less differentiated patriarchal societies, in which authority may have been called "father," such authority represented something more than a familial symbol.[48]

Erikson's approach, then, is characterized by an explicit awareness of social structure, to which individual dynamics are related; changes at the social level will affect personal dynamics in various ways. This approach was employed by Erikson, for example, in his works on Luther and Gandhi. However, though Erikson's work is grounded in social events, he has actually said little about the nature and character of social structure in a systematic way. When he has addressed himself to historical problems, therefore, he has pretty much limited his work to the analysis of individuals.[49]

[48] Talcott Parsons, "The Father Symbol" and "The Incest Taboo," *Social Structure and Personality* (Glencoe, Ill., 1964), pp. 51–52, 67, 75.

[49] Erikson has made much broader sociological statements. In *Childhood and Society*, for example (pp. 292–94), he wrote that the mother in the American family had to become more libidinally removed from her children, she had to develop ego and superego motives that would enable her to direct her children to tolerate the pressures imposed by a highly mobile and rapidly changing frontier society. But Erikson has not investigated such problems in a systematic way.

In sum, there has developed in psychoanalytic theory a strong sense of the distinctiveness of particular historical periods, of the differences that distinguish one time and place from another. It is also quite justified, in terms of psychoanalytic theory as it has evolved, to accord social-structural factors a primary place in the analysis of social and psychological change.[50] Thus, historical data can be viewed from a standpoint that integrates sociological and psychoanalytic theory. In fact, the two approaches are intimately connected with each other and with the study of history. Without the sociological dimension it is very difficult to explain social change; and without psychoanalytic theory the variety of human responses to social change cannot be explained in any comprehensive way.

[50] See R. S. Wallerstein and N. J. Smelser, "Psychoanalysis and Sociology: Articulations and Applications," *Int. J. Psychoanal.*, 50 (1969): 694.

II. *An Integrated Approach*

In a very significant sense, the appearance of Erikson's *Childhood and Society*, and then the publication of other of his works on Luther and Gandhi, not only gave to psychoanalysis a much wider and more attentive public, but also gave to the academic pursuit of history and sociology a reason for attending to psychoanalytic insight. Those familiar with psychoanalytic interpretations of historical and social events realize that Erikson's comments in *Childhood and Society* on such figures as Hitler and Gorky represent a break and a bridge. The psychosocial frame of reference, and the stress on object relations, which tie the individual through his "caretaking" persons to the wider social world, gave to historical and sociological workers a basis for analysis and investigation which had hitherto largely been missing from psychoanalytic endeavor.

We can make more explicit what Erikson attempted by examining briefly certain problems that Freud faced, and the kind of solution he typically achieved. Consider, for example, Freud's analysis of the vicissitudes of oedipal conflict. If the boy loves his mother and hates his father, how is it that the boy identifies with his father and not with his mother? Freud had learned from his study of mourning and melancholia that identification arises from the renunciation of a loved object, a factor which would point to an identification with the mother. That is, "owing to a real slight or disappointment coming from this loved person, the object-relationship was shattered. . . . The object cathexis proved to have little power of resistance and was brought to an end. But the free libido was not displaced on to another object; it was withdrawn into the ego. There, however, it was not employed in any unspecified way, but seemed to establish an identification of the ego with the abandoned object."[1] In order to resolve this seeming contradiction, Freud postulated a situation of constitutional bisexuality; the boy also loves his father and hates his mother, and in the resolution of the oedipal crisis he identifies with both parents.

[1] Freud, "Mourning and Melancholia," 14: 249.

Still, it is clear that the boy identifies with his father to a much greater degree than with his mother. It is possible to say that the continued pursuit of libidinal gratifications raises the fear of castration, and so the boy's ultimate behavior is biologically and psychologically guaranteed. Indeed, the more Freud thought about the problem, the more convinced he became that the fear of the castrating father is the primary motive for the dissolution of the Oedipus complex and for the development of the consequent identifications. But the profound alterations of character which are implied in the resolution of the Oedipus complex must be based on something more positive than identification with an aggressor. Other psychoanalytic writers reviewing this problem have suggested in addition that even before the oedipal crisis there has been a considerable degree of ego development which facilitates the process of growth: "The oedipal crisis has been preceded by a long history of renunciation, and of building up inner controls, capacity for delay, reality testing, and relatively neutralized interests."[2] Furthermore, psychoanalysts have also taken into account the influence of environment: "For the boy the masculine identification usually possesses greater adaptive and synthesizing utility than the feminine, and it customarily receives more environmental support."[3]

These suggestions are clearly more encompassing than Freud's original ideas on bisexuality and castration. The instinctual motives for renunciation are still of the utmost importance,[4] but the addition of ego and environmental factors allows for a more balanced and comprehensive view. For one thing this means that the boy must have gotten positive support from his father, who would then appear to him as something more than the punitive representative of reality. It is in these terms that a sociological view of these processes becomes useful. Parsons has written, for example,

> that some of the principal facts which Freud interpreted as manifestations of constitutional bisexuality can be explained by the fact that the categorization of human persons—including the actor's categorization of himself taken as a point of reference—into two sexes is not,

[2] Roy Schafer, *Aspects of Internalization* (New York, 1968), p. 207.
[3] *Ibid.*, p. 183.
[4] *Ibid.*, p. 208. "When the boy modifies his ego motives and behavior patterns and self-representations along the lines laid down by his father's character, he is all at once expressing (1) his fear of his father and of object loss (castration anxiety), (2) his hateful wish to replace his father so as to satisfy his possessive, erotic desire for his mother, and (3) his sexual, affectionate admiring feelings toward his father. Corresponding features exist with regard to his identification with his mother."

except in its somatic points of reference, biologically given, but, in psychological significance, must be learned by the child. It is fundamental that children of both sexes start life with essentially the same relation to the mother, a fact on which Freud himself rightly laid great stress. It may then be suggested that the process by which the boy learns to differentiate himself in terms of sex from the mother and in this sense "identify" with the father, while the girl learns to identify with the mother, *is a learning process.* One major part of the process of growing up is the internalization of one's own sex role as a critical part of the self-image. It may well be that this way of looking at the process will have the advantage of making the assumption of constitutional bisexuality at least partly superfluous as an explanation of the individual's sex identification. In any case it has the great advantage of linking the determination of sex categorizations directly with the role structure of the social system in a theoretical as well as an empirical sense.[5]

Thus, without doing violence to psychoanalytic theory, the sociological formulation, by emphasizing the ego and environmental factors, explains at the same time how individuals are integrated into specific social structures. The identification and internalization processes are learning processes: "With the development of the capacity to form the first object relationship, knowledge of the environment will also be acquired culturally."[6] Freud's emphasis on bisexuality, no matter how important it may be in certain respects, is not an adequate basis for an explanation of identification and the formation of superego. On the one hand, it can be said that "Freud attempted to answer this question in what seems to have been for him a hurried manner."[7] But, on the other hand, it must be said that at crucial points Freud chose the biopsychological, anatomical, and/or constitutional explanation when explanation in ego and social terms would have made more sense.

We can take as another example a problem related to this one, the ability of the woman to function at the social level in systematic ego and superego terms. Having identified castration anxiety as a motive for the resolution of oedipal conflict, Freud had to insist that there were differences between the sexes with regard to superego development in these terms. Castration anxiety cannot have the same effect on girls that it has

---

[5] Talcott Parsons, *Social Structure and Personality* (Glencoe, Ill., 1964), p. 26; italics added. See also Schafer, *Aspects of Internalization*, p. 158; and Edith Jacobson, "The Self and the Object World," *Pyschoanal. Stud. Child*, 9 (1954): 119–20.

[6] Arnold H. Modell, *Object Love and Reality* (New York, 1968), p. 159.

[7] Schafer, *Aspects of Internalization*, p. 197.

on boys; boys renounce the oedipal conflict much more decisively, and consequently make much stronger superego identifications.

I cannot evade the notion (though I hesitate to give it expression) that for women what is ethically normal is different from what it is in men. Their superego is never so inexorable, so impersonal, so independent of its emotional origins as we require it to be in men. Character traits which critics of every epoch have brought up against women—that they show less sense of justice than men, that they are less ready to submit to the great exigencies of life, that they are more often influenced in their judgments by feelings of affection and hostility—all these would be amply accounted for by the modifications in the formation of their superego which we have inferred above.[8]

Women, therefore, are more tied to the immediate give-and-take of real relations, they remain at the (lower) developmental level of the wish to be loved or the fear of the loss of love. Women cannot manage the emotional constraint that leads to effective self-control and hence to abstract modes of dealing with the environment. Women cannot be as independent or autonomous as men. Freud wrote that "women represent the interests of family and of sexual life. The work of civilization has become increasingly the business of men, it confronts them with ever more difficult tasks and compels them to carry out instinctual sublimations of which women are little capable."[9]

Freud's judgment was based on his observation of, and experience with, a certain type of dependent behavior among females, and this experience is not being questioned. What is being questioned is Freud's explanation of this behavior; that is, did the dependence stem from immutable bio-psychological factors, or from social-structural factors, which are manifestly subject to change? From a contemporary perspective we can state that one really cannot identify in given instances any ego or superego qualities that would inhibit female success, say, in business or politics. Moreover, if women prove capable of organizing a social movement—as they now seem in the process of doing—and the movement is characterized by the same ego and superego qualities that Freud ascribed to men, the differences he identified could not possibly have been in the biopsychological factors. The differences would have to have been in social-structural factors.

Once again, as with earlier examples, it is not that Freud was entirely unaware of the ways in which society may affect behavior; he wrote that

[8] Freud, "Some Psychical Consequences of the Anatomical Distinction between the Sexes," 19: 257–58.

[9] Freud, "Civilization and Its Discontents," 21: 103.

"we must beware . . . of underestimating the influence of social customs, which . . . force women into a passive situation."[10] And Freud's last formulation of the superego and identification concepts was much more comprehensive and sociological than earlier ones. He wrote that "in all this it is not only the personal qualities of their parents that is making itself felt, but also everything that had a determining effect on them themselves, the tastes and standards of the social class in which they lived and the innate dispositions and traditions of the race from which they sprang."[11] But preponderantly Freud was convinced of the inevitability of the female's position in society because of the anatomical and psychological factors.[12]

We have now identified three instances (i.e., adolescence and both male and female types of identification and resolution of oedipal conflict) in which sociologically oriented explanations make more sense and explain more data than Freud's original statements, which were basically psychological in their thrust. These three instances represent points of weakness in the explanatory power of the theory, and they are also instances which can be empirically investigated. However, what we mean in the broadest terms is that explanations which systematically involve social-structural factors can be extended and applied over the full range of psychoanalytic concern, eliminating thereby the inherently ahistorical posture of traditional psychoanalysis.

Erikson's work, then, must be viewed in these terms; it represents an attempt to add a sociological dimension to psychoanalysis. But Erikson has not gone far enough in this direction. To be sure, Erikson indicates that individuals are formed by the particular social structures in which they develop, and that the process of formation is continuous through

---

[10] Freud, "New Introductory Lectures on Psychoanalysis," 22: 116.

[11] Freud, "An Outline of Psychoanalysis," 23: 206.

[12] Psychoanalysts are themselves subject to distortion on the basis of resistance and other factors. This stems from the fact that psychoanalysts are, like everyone else, rooted in a sociological position which makes insight into certain problems difficult. We have already noted Ruth Mack Brunswick's comments on psychoanalytic resistance to the preoedipal concept (see p. 50, n. 30). On Freud's bias with regard to women, see, e. g., Martin H. Stein, "The Problem of Character Theory," *J. Amer. Psychoanal. Ass.*, 17, no. 3 (July, 1969): 687. On the problem of women, social background, and changing psychoanalytic views, see Robert Seidenberg, "The Trauma of Eventlessness," *Psychoanal. Rev.*, 59, no. 1 (Spring, 1972): 95–109. For other psychoanalytic observations on resistance among psychoanalysts themselves, see, e.g., Jacobson, "The Self and the Object World," p. 118; *idem*, "Development of the Wish for a Child in Boys," *Psychoanal. Stud. Child*, 5 (1950): 144; Norman B. Atkins, "The Oedipus Myth, Adolescence, and the Succession of Generations," *J. Amer. Psychoanal. Ass.*, 18, no. 4 (October, 1970): 862–63, 871; George Devereaux, "The Cannibal Impulses of Parents," *Psychoanalytic Forum*, 1 (1966): 114.

the life cycle. But Erikson does not draw out or make explicit the implications of this observation, and this is most evident in his analysis of persons who have rebelled against the internalized mandates of their society. Erikson still remains too much bound by the psychoanalytic ontogenetic and familial models.

Erikson's analysis of a film in his chapter on Gorky (*Childhood and Society*) is a good starting point for an examination of this problem. The connections and interpretations here, a display of an unmatched mastery of this theoretical and clinical approach, are particularly interesting. To refresh our memories, the essential theme of the Gorky piece is the development of a youth in traditional Russian society, the meeting and passing of a series of opportunities which, if seized, could lead to independence, but, if allowed to pass, or if misinterpreted, would lead to dependence and to the compliant acceptance of traditional bondage. Erikson describes the gap between the given and the emergent, the traditional and the evolutionary—on the one hand, "a cyclic personality structure characterized by apathetic drudgery, childlike trust, sudden outbursts of consuming passions, and a sense of depressing doom," and, on the other hand, a new frame of mind in which what counts is "critical caution, incorruptible patience, absolute avoidance of wrong action, the ripening of clear inner direction, and then—action."[13]

At one point, Erikson comments on an episode in the film, an encounter between a radical and the young boy, in which the boy is urged to "take life," in this context meaning not to endure it but to grasp and master it, and without a bad conscience, which might come from a sense of transgression. This determined "grasping," Erikson says, paired with a resistance against sinking back into dependence, "is of outstanding importance in Bolshevik psychology." This is a critical passage because it moves from the individual to the group. But it is a passage that presents us with problems because, while we think it is correct, we wonder how Erikson got from the one entity to the other, from the problems of a youth to Russian and Bolshevik problems. What theoretical justification is there for this leap? In fact, aside from the appeal the insight of a master has for us, there is no justification for it.[14]

The Luther work, too, presents us with a combination of peerless clinical insight and tenuous sociological suggestion. Erikson goes much further than the others, but still not far enough. That is, Luther may have his problems, but he is not presented in that ineffably trite psychoanalytic fashion which involves explaining why some neurotic is fighting an

---

[13] Erik Erikson, *Childhood and Society*, 2d ed. (New York, 1963), pp. 398, 382.
[14] *Ibid.*, pp. 384–85.

institutional authority when he should more appropriately be home fighting with his father. In Luther, psychic, social, and cultural events are interwoven, personal experience and social strain are related to each other. The Church in significant ways had failed, and the existence of other social tensions, along with problems in the Church, created a situation in which Luther's personal dynamics could become the focal point for a mass movement.

This analysis is important because it points to the reality factors involved in Luther's struggle; society is not seen merely as a screen on which fantasies and wishes are projected, an arena in which people fight out the unresolved conflicts of their personal past. On this basis we could never understand why Luther became such a powerful leader. Demands for change predicated on idiosyncratically expressed wishes could never provide the impetus for mass action, for the mobilization of a class or nation. We are familiar now with the idea of "the return of the repressed," and have already asked what this can mean in a social context. Repression may fail at any time in any given instance and take the form of symptoms or, sublimated or displaced, it may take the form of an ideological gesture. But what can this mean for other people whose defenses are intact? How can others experience as important what one insists must be important on the basis of idiosyncratic experience?

Erikson's emphasis, of course, is on Luther, but why or how it was that Luther attracted a mass following is not explained. It is clear that Luther was an imposing leader, just as it is clear that Erikson's analysis of dependence and autonomy is a central feature in Bolshevik imagination. But the question still remains: How can we interpret the behavior of the group and explain the relationship of the leader to the led? We may agree that people do act in concert and that very often this action is not explicable in terms of conscious self- or class-interested behavior. It is easy to point to crucial examples of mass behavior which only psychoanalytic insight into rage or devotion can illuminate. Parsimony dictates that an attempt be made to integrate psychoanalytic insight into sociological explanation. Erikson summed up the need, but he did not elaborate the method.

As we have noted, one way that writers have approached such a problem has been to assume that an innovator's or activist's biography was not unique, but was shared by many others at the same time in the same way. This is still the essential thrust of Erikson's psychosocial analysis. Specific societies and the "caretaking" representatives of these societies organize experience for the young, who are integrated into given patterns of giving and taking, competing and cooperating. The central institutional focus of this socialization process is the family, and analysis is based on ontogenetic development in a familial structure geared to the mandates of a still wider world. Internalization of norms, values, and standards takes place in the context of a highly emotional, intense relationship which guarantees stability and establishes the basis for further growth.

However, when we deal with men like Gorky and Luther, we are dealing with violators of the given mandates and not with those who seek their fulfillment. Moreover, we are dealing with types of behavior and ideological commitments which have no structured past and no legitimation in the societies in which they occurred. The very names that Erikson has given to certain stages of life—i.e., autonomy, initiative—have no meaning in the modern sense to the societies in which these men developed. We can understand that a basic sense of trust is always crucial for future action, and in that sense the ontogenetic-familial scheme is relevant. But where did the revolutionary content come from, and from what did the impetus for radical change derive? How were men mobilized for transgression? There is an implicit contradiction here between the ontogenetic-familial model and the circumstances of radical change. The one is most useful for demonstrating how people are integrated in a society and why they may want to stay in; the other raises questions about how and why people get out. When we get down to cases, a model based on the development of the individual in the family is not an adequate one for explaining the kind of revolutionary events Erikson chose to deal with.

What we are suggesting with these comments is that, for a man like Luther to appear *and to command obedience and loyalty*, there must somehow be an independent—a relatively independent—relationship between social structure and personality dynamics. Moreover, this is more fundamental than is indicated either by classic psychoanalytic theory or by Erikson's psychosocial contributions, which still tie the actor to the wider world largely through the family. For various reasons there was originally in psychoanalytic endeavor a radical devaluation of the external world, meaning specifically a devaluation of political, economic, and other such social structures. Erikson identified this and tried to integrate this level of reality into psychoanalytic thought. But the most valuable suggestions in Erikson are still only implicit, and what is required is, explicitly, a psychoanalytic sociology.

In other words, if Erikson still presents us with difficulties because of his emphasis on personal and familial dynamics, there are crucial suggestions in his work which point to certain connections between social and psychic structures and which can be of great help to us. We refer in particular to Erikson's analysis of psychosocial development as a continuous ongoing process which he has organized into eight stages. In Erikson's view, as we know, there are critical conflicts that individuals must resolve in each stage—i.e., opportunities for integrated advancement, but possibilities for regressive experience as well. It is justified to assume, therefore, that identity is not a fixed, static quality, but is continually being challenged and requires definition and perhaps redefinition at each stage in life.[15] What Erikson suggests is that people are continuously interacting with their environment (physical, symbolic, social, personal), and that no resolution of conflict at any point is necessarily an irreversible one.

By contrast, the classic psychoanalytic position fixed the formation of personality in the early childhood phases too rigidly. The basis on which this occurred—in the early days of extraordinary discoveries—is not difficult to determine. There are a number of continually encountered assumptions in the psychoanalytic literature which point inevitably to the traditional conclusions. Thus, one reads that a man never relinquishes a libidinal position; when he appears to give something up, all he really does is adopt a substitute. Further, the finding of an object is really only the refinding of one; and the object is what is most variable about a drive. What all this adds up to is the primacy of infantile and early childhood experiences and of family relationships. From this point, as we have seen, it was logical enough to conclude that various external authorities are a reproduction of familial types of authority, and that such a social event as revolution really changes nothing fundamental with regard to personality and behavior.[16]

Contemporary psychoanalytic writers have found it necessary to withdraw from this position. The weight of pre- and postoedipal influences on

---

[15] Identity is a difficult and complex concept, but for the sake of the present argument let us say that it refers to a complex interplay between bodily, psychological, and social processes which reaches a crucial point at the end of adolescence, an interplay which is the source of conflict that must be resolved in a successful synthesis of the variety of potential "choices" the individual has in defining what he is and what he will be. One result of this synthesis must be a stable sense of self, characterized by a feeling of "sameness and continuity." Moreover, consistent with Erikson's assumption that there is coordination between the developing individual and his social environment (mutuality), society is understood to provide the institutional setting within which identity problems can be resolved. Erikson's concept of identity implies the bringing together within the individual of the multiple and complex social roles that one has played and will continue to play. The present importance of the concept and the widespread awareness of it have more specific implications—namely, the existence of a society in which multiple roles, open-ended choices, and personal responsibility for choices are not only possible and permissible but obligatory. This leads to anxiety, but also to awareness.

[16] See, e.g., Gregory Rochlin, *Griefs and Discontents* (Boston, 1965), pp. 98, 122, 196.

behavior and character formation cannot be gotten around.[17] A variety of observations (including, for example, Piaget's observations on cognitive development) led to the need to redefine the conditions under which character development takes place. The most important of these relate to adolescent conflicts. Psychoanalysts' systematic awareness of the problems of adolescence is recent enough for Hartmann to have written that the potentialities for the transformation of personality throughout latency and adolescence have been underrated in psychoanalytic work.[18] But by now the problems of adolescent development and conflict have been thoroughly integrated in psychoanalytic imagination, and we are not surprised when certain resolutions formerly ascribed solely to the oedipal phase are now ascribed to the adolescent period: "Adolescence is the final period of development for the resolution of incestuous wishes, and an opportunity for the 'neutralization' of drive energy hitherto directed toward the cathexis of original love objects."[19]

[17] On the preoedipal period and possible sociological and historical implications for authority relationships and structures, see Charles H. Kramer, ed., "Maxwell Gitelson: Analytic Aphorisms," *Psychoanal. Quart.*, 36, no. 2 (1967): 264; Charles N. Sarlin, "The Concept of Genital Primacy," *J. Amer. Psychoanal. Ass.*, 18, no. 2 (April, 1970): 291–93; and *idem*, "Identity, Culture, and Psychosexual Development," *American Imago*, 24, no. 3 (Fall, 1967): 181–247. See also, Marian Tolpin, "The Infantile Neurosis," *Psychoanal. Stud. Child*, 25 (1970): 276; Irving Shuren, "A Contribution to the Metapsychology of the Preanalytic Patient," *ibid.*, 22 (1967); and Sandor Lorand, "Psycho-Analytic Therapy of Religious Devotees," *Int. J. Psychoanal.*, 43 (January–February, 1962): 54. In historical and sociological terms, see David Hunt, *Parents and Children in History* (New York, 1970), pp. 152–58, 178, 191–95; F. Weinstein and G. M. Platt, *The Wish To Be Free* (Berkeley and Los Angeles, 1970), chap. 7.

[18] H. Hartmann, E. Kris, and R. M. Loewenstein, "The Formation of Psychic Structure," *Papers*, pp. 51, 35. Note also the following statement: "How are we to explain the timing of actual character formation? Appeals to some inferred special characteristics of oedipal or other developmental phases really cannot explain this question. Anal problems are certainly just as intense, the anxieties of this period are just as severe, identifications with parents are obviously made which involve efforts at prohibitions of drives, and yet character is not formed with the resolution of this psychosexual stage. One can argue that the oedipal stage is unique and different from earlier stages, but the oedipal crisis is at its height at ages three to five and character formation is not evident at this time in childhood." Irving Steingart, "On Self, Character, and the Development of a Psychic Apparatus," *Psychoanal. Stud. Child*, 24 (1969): 283, 284–85.

[19] Z. Alexander Aarons, "Normality and Abnormality in Adolescence," *Psychoanal. Stud. Child*, 25 (1970): 318. One way of looking at the problem is that, as social change has affected the socialization process, different age levels have become involved in an intensity of conflict that had earlier been typically associated with early childhood. And different institutions beyond the family have become involved in such conflict. In Freud's day, for example, the oedipal stage and the family were a crucial time and place of conflict. At present, however, it seems to us that the oedipal period presents less of a problem (in terms of the society; individuals may certainly still be seriously affected), but late adolescence and early adulthood and the educational establishment have become a crucial time and place of conflict. The origin and timing of problems change, and not everything begins and ends in the individual and/or the family.

But even this view cannot be fully reconciled with historical and sociological data and with the implications of Erikson's work. It does not take into account Erikson's description of stages and resolutions of conflict after adolescence and the identity crisis. Furthermore, it does not take into account or describe adequately the causes and effects of revolutionary activity, and we cannot insist upon this point too strongly—that is, social-structural events can interrupt an "average expectable environment" at any time and force an identity crisis and a redefinition of the world. There is no point in saying that adolescence is the final period for the resolution of incestuous wishes when we know that revolutionaries, no matter what their age, must meet and resolve this problem. In addition, this view does not take into account sufficiently certain developments in personality which can most readily be identified in modern, pluralized societies. There is more flexibility and possibility for change than was stated or implied in the traditional psychoanalytic position, a position which Erikson managed greatly to improve.

What we are suggesting with these remarks is that a variety of concepts, such as internalization, identification, object relations, and so on, have been too narrowly defined and interpreted and this has led to a less dynamic view of social process and social change than is warranted by evidence. Identification processes do not stop with childhood or adolescence. Freud understood this and commented on it; indeed, he stated that the later identifications "regularly make important contributions to the formation of character." But Freud limited the effects of this process to ego, concluding that superego was not affected. However, in view of the structural position that any action has meaning for all levels of the personality (the principle of multiple function), Waelder observed some time ago that superego can be modified "even in the third decade of life." The structuralization of ego and superego does not imply subsequent fixity.[20]

Identity is comprised of internalized features, but identity must also be re-established and can be redefined throughout life. Ego and superego processes which are established in childhood are not static; they expand and contract. The capacity for reality testing, which increases with age, and the need to examine and re-examine ideals and values in late adolescence, to cite an example we have already introduced, is indicative of this. "These later encounters with the environment are influenced by conditions and issues that were not even differentiated in the child's mind at the time of superego formation either because they were not relevant or

[20] See Henri Parens and Leon J. Saul, *Dependence in Man* (New York, 1971), p. 50, on Freud and Waelder. See also H. Nagera, "The Concepts of Structure and Structuralization," *Psychoanal. Stud. Child*, 22 (1967): 94–95.

because they require a perspective of which the young child is incapable."[21] Such encounters, however, may occur and recur at every age level, and this is why Erikson's notion of stages and his observation that the successful resolution of crisis in any stage of life does not guarantee the continued stability of that resolution are important. They lead to the conclusion that, in a broader sense, *social-structural changes which affect the implementation of values and norms in a society can affect any and all age levels, systematically engendering redefinition of self and others.*

The more pluralized a society is, the truer it is that normative depictions of self and others are liable to change. In modern pluralized societies individuals are continually involved in defining their identity in a variety of social situations. "Observation shows that *to some extent and within limits* people with highly developed moral standards continuously redefine what is moral and estimable about themselves in terms of what the environment appears to recognize, accept and reward."[22] However, because of the depth and extent of certain types of social change (i.e., change that leads to the violation of the morality that binds interaction and that interferes with ego standards for achievement and drive gratification), people may decathect ("desacralize") a given set of standards and expectations and redefine these whether society approves or not. The individual's attachment to internalized patterns of behavior must be viewed in relation to actual current conditions, but also in relation to new types of experience. This latter relationship between internalized standards and new types of experience is the cardinal factor in revolutionary behavior. It is true, of course, that such behavior may come to be regressive, particularly in that the connection between identifications and original (infantile) figures and motives may become excessively important again, and lead to various distortions of reality. But this is not an inevitable result, and identifications may be supported by figures and motives other than the original ones.

The need to exercise personal control over wider and more diverse cultural and social contents is one of the dominant characteristics of a highly pluralized society, just as the standards that define the conditions under which change can occur are characterized by greater flexibility. This means that individuals act in terms of a variety of mandates, but

---

[21] Roy Schafer, "Ideals, Ego Ideal, and Ideal Self," in *Motives and Thought: Essays in Honor of David Rapaport*, ed. R. R. Holt, Psychological Issues, no. 18/19 (New York, 1967), pp. 168, 171–72, 137–38. Modell, *Object Love and Reality*, pp. 121, 135; Peter Blos, "Character Formation in Adolescence," *Psychoanal. Stud. Child*, 23 (1968): 248; *idem*, "The Second Individuation Process of Adolescence," *ibid.*, 22 (1967): 182–83.

[22] Roy Schafer, *Aspects of Internalization* (New York, 1968), p. 157; *idem*, "Ideals, Ego Ideal and Ideal Self," pp. 132, 135; see also Robert Jay Lifton's position, which is similar, in "Protean Man," *History and Human Survival* (New York, 1970), pp. 311–31.

they are also engaged in thinking about and interpreting these mandates, and in deciding how and when to act on them. In terms of this latter situation we can say that people "know" when social mandates are unjust, or when a given morality is being violated, or when given standards for achievement cannot be acted upon, and they make decisions about change. However, it must be emphasized that, while this situation is more generalized in more pluralized societies, it has always existed to some degree. No known society is totally undifferentiated—that is, is not differentiated at least on the basis of age and sex. But, when such differentiation exists, ego and superego capacities must also exist to define behavior along these lines. Therefore, even in the most primitive societies violation of the patterns of behavior which bind action will be responded to by demands for the redress of grievances. This is the paramount factor in considerations of social change.[23]

The internalization of objects, ideals, and values, of normative mandates and prohibitions, of patterns and contents of behavior, which define the relationship of self to others, is not a once-and-forever phenomenon. The relationship between the individual and society is *produced;* it is established initially and must be re-established continually over time. That is, internalized mandates are not the sole determinants of action: internalized dictates must combine with ego controls and reality testing, social-structural exigencies and opportunities, social and cultural direc-

---

[23] W. E. H. Stanner speaks of a "one possibility thing" regarding Australian aboriginal religious modes of interpreting the world. This comes closest to an undifferentiated situation. But differentiation with regard to age, sex, and kinship has been observed among these people too, so that some degree of choice must be involved, no matter how narrow it may be. W. E. H. Stanner, "The Dreaming," in *Reader in Comparative Religion*, ed. W. Lessa and E. Z. Vogt (New York, 1965), pp. 153–67. The point made here is important for psychosocial analyses of historical events, and it relates to the third of our qualifications above, the effects of the modernization process on personality. That is, we can identify historically a growing capacity among individuals for making conscious, ego-oriented choices. This is limited randomly by the inadequacies and failures of individuals, and systematically by the boundaries established by the societies in which this capacity has evolved. In connection with this we can identify also an increasing level of conscious control over the morality that organizes behavior in a variety of situations. In brief, individuals are able to review their "thoughts, feelings, and actions from several points of view, including the moral, rather than being overwhelmed by the moral point of view alone; furthermore, this moral point of view . . . is articulated partly with a moral code that is somewhat independent of superego functions." Schafer, *Aspects of Internalization*, p. 106. This means that the process of examination and definition of values and identity, and the capacity for redefinition of identity, is true for all people in their prosaic, everyday lives. It is for such reasons as these that psychic processes are better understood in relation to the specific social situations in which they have occurred, and in terms of the historical background from which they have evolved.

tives, and so on. The result of this is a potential for social and personal change at any point in time.

Technically speaking, anxiety can result from intrapsychic (drive) conflict, but anxiety can also be experienced when disrupted social conditions threaten the adequacy of ego's efforts to integrate cognitive, perceptual, and other functions with changing reality, making action difficult or ineffective. In such situations people attempt to bring the environment back under control, to make the environment intelligible and satisfying in one way or another. The consequent behaviors may be regressive (in clinical terms, rigid, automatic, dependent upon external authority, etc.), but, by the same token, the self can be redefined successfully so that the individual can act in new and autonomous ways and develop new social situations.[24] This process is easier to identify in the great men in history, particularly in the charismatic leaders, but it is not applicable only to them.

Thus, in the more traditional psychoanalytic terms it may be argued that "the superego cannot be remodeled, reorganized, and consolidated; new personal and sexual relations, new ego structures and functions cannot be built up and integrated unless these new formations are allowed to grow organically from those of the past."[25] However, this is not an adequate descriptive basis for interpreting behavior when, for example, the values and norms of society dictate a tolerance for change; and it most certainly is not descriptively accurate for revolutionary situations.[26] Such a state-

[24] George S. Klein, "On Hearing One's Own Voice," in *Drives, Affects, Behavior*, ed. Max Schur, 2 vols. (New York, 1965), 2: 90. To be more specific, it is true that conflict between an individual or group and some institutional structure external to the family can bring oedipal conflicts to the surface again. The anxiety and guilt provoked by conflict may lead to regressive forms of behavior in oedipal or even preoedipal terms. But it is also true that institutions can become dysfunctional in terms of psychic- and social-structural developments and that an attack against such an institution can be justified in terms of psychic economics—i.e., guilt and anxiety will be minimal, ego-oriented control will be manifest, and the figures attacked will be the ones provoking strain and will not be merely symbols for transferred and inappropriate feelings that relate to the familial past.

[25] Edith Jacobson, "Adolescent Moods and the Remodeling of Psychic Structure in Adolescence," *Psychoanal. Stud. Child*, 16 (1961): 169. Because of the behavior changes that can occur with revolutionary activity we would say that such a formulation is, theoretically speaking, too cautious.

[26] The fact that the values and norms mandate a tolerance for change leads to problems at the level of therapy, as we noted before. In particular, the two factors of ego-oriented choice and some control over the morality that binds situations are important goals of therapy in modern society; all of these factors are sociologically interrelated. "[In] successful therapy, the flexible discriminatory functions of the ego, which in the adult are potentially under control and therefore capable of rationality, will regain some of the selective freedom that had been lost to the id through sexualization and aggressivization and to the superego by institutionalization." F. J. Hacker, "The

ment is useful for us in the sense that changes in ego interests and superego mandates are not likely to occur in regard to every institutional level, and the continued stability of some part of the structure facilitates change in other parts; and in the sense that it is likely that some unconscious fantasies will have been cathected, refined, and brought into line in an ideological sense with changed social circumstances. These qualifications, however, are not sufficient to contradict the essential point, which is that men can redefine and refashion identities and institute novel patterns of behavior. Of course, this never happens without conflict—and the function of the charismatic leader may be understood in these terms: the charismatic leader attempts to facilitate a transition to new patterns of behavior which have *not* been developed organically from the past but which are, by contrast, more or less appropriate solutions to the conditions and situations individuals are currently facing.

To a significant extent these conclusions are implicit in Erikson's work; the sociological variables are evident just beneath the surface. Robert Bellah has pointed out that "Erikson also contributed to the broader problem of religious change by indicating that Luther's solution, once it was embodied in communicable symbolic form, could be appropriated by others in the same society that had analogous identity problems arising from *social-historical* matrices similar to Luther's own." What we are insisting upon is an emphasis on the social-historical events and not necessarily upon the individual—that is, to stress in a systematic way the sociological background to ideology and action, employing individual instances as examples, but not viewing the individual as the fundamental problem.[27]

One other important factor must be examined in the given context and this is the different levels at which society affects and structures personality. The starting point for this must be Freud's theory of superego, which provided the initial link between psychoanalytic and sociological theory. Freud, of course, understood the moral mandates internalized in superego to be binding and to represent the chief stabilizing factor in the individual's relationship to the social order. Moreover, as we have indi-

---

Discriminatory Function of the Ego," *Int. J. Psychoanal.*, 43 (November–December, 1962): 401. Furthermore, the analyst can help his patients by "uncovering their adherence to the severe parental demands, thus enabling the mature person to *choose his own norms and restrictions in a healthier way.*" Jeanne Lampl–de Groot, "On Obstacles Standing in the Way of Psychoanalytic Cure," *Psychoanal. Stud. Child*, 23 (1967): 22–23; italics added. See also Martin H. Stein, "Self-Observation, Reality, and the Superego," in *Psychoanalysis: A General Psychology*, ed. R. M. Loewenstein *et al.*, p. 288.

[27] Robert Bellah, *Beyond Belief: Essays on Religion in a Post-Traditional World* (New York, 1970); italics added.

cated, in his late definition of the problem, Freud pursued a rather sociological orientation—that is, he noted that the child is affected not only by the personalities of the parents but also by "the family, racial and national traditions handed on through them, as well as the demands of the immediate social *milieu* which they represent."

Extending this line of reasoning, Parsons has suggested that more than superego must be affected in these terms in order to account adequately for the formation of personality and for social stability; internalization and identification cannot be conceived of as limited to the superego. Parsons concludes, then, that actually three different dimensions of interaction are internalized—namely, the cognitive and affectual, as well as the moral. That is, the way in which two or more people view each other includes a definition of what each person is (the cognitive function, as with regard to status, for example) and what each means to the other in an emotional sense (the affectual function), while the standards of moral evaluation serve to bind action, in the sense that cognitive and affectual meanings are held constant over time. These patterns provide the background which actors rely upon to organize behavior with regard to each other and in order to achieve a basis of consensus with regard to such behavior. Further, these patterns are culturally learned, but this learning is not left to chance. As societies are presently organized, therefore, these patterns are learned and fixed in the highly emotional familial context and are continually enforced both within the family and the wider social world.[28]

In Parsons's view all aspects of the personality are linked to society and culture in these terms. For example, ego is not developed solely through interaction with the external world but is developed also through the internalization of normative patterns of behavior. However, from this standpoint, id impulses also are understood to comprise a symbolically generalized system. The reality experience of the individual and the cultural patterns he has learned (via identification) affect even the most primitive and least organized processes of the psychic apparatus, lending structure to them. Interestingly enough, any number of psychoanalysts have come to a similar position on the nature of id processes; and one psychoanalyst, Roy Schafer, has explicitly organized a position very similar to Parsons's in a number of respects, but particularly with regard to the definition of ego and id processes.[29]

---

[28] Parsons, *Social Structure and Personality*, pp. 20–21. Freud's theory of superego converges with Durkheim's ideas on stability in a social system. Parsons considers that this convergence "deserves to be ranked as one of the truly fundamental landmarks of the development of modern social science" (*ibid.*, p. 19). The quote from Freud is from "An Outline of Psychoanalysis," 23: 146.

[29] Schafer, "Ideals, Ego Ideal, and Ideal Self," pp. 131–74; on the problem of the id, see esp. p. 147, n. 13.

With regard to ego, Schafer states that functions, interests, and standards develop to a significant extent

> in relation to parental care and example. The observing parent is not merely someone who opposes instinctual expression and fosters renunciation . . . (Identification with these aspects of the parent is at the center of superego formation). The observing parent also provides, teaches, and supports effective modes of ego activity, serving in this respect as an auxiliary ego. Simultaneously, the maturing child cannot fail to observe the parent's ego activities in many aspects of life and to be deeply influenced by his observations. Since the parent's activities and child-rearing practices inevitably express his own ego functions, interests, and standards (which, in their specific forms, are also more or less those of his culture), he continuously provides models and encourages the child to develop similar ego characteristics.[30]

With regard to id processes Schafer states that the development and strengths of the various id tendencies *are influenced by identifications*, and included in these id-centered identifications are "the standards or ideals held by the parental ego for these id tendencies." Further, Freud wrote in *The Ego and the Id* that "it dawns upon us like a new discovery that only something which has once been a [conscious] perception can become conscious, and that anything from within (apart from feelings) that seeks to become conscious must try to transform itself into external perceptions: this becomes possible by means of memory-traces." In other words, the id includes the *repressed* unconscious; wishes rejected by ego and superego tendencies are wishes elaborated in cultural terms. The id concept "refers not simply to an aggregate of ideationally unelaborated instinctual tendencies"; "Freud's definition of the id as including the repressed unconscious can only mean that it includes perceptions, images, concepts, and memories pertaining to the self and objects."[31]

To readers generally aware of Freud's ideas on id processes this may seem a rather surprising conclusion. In Freud's most famous definition, the id was conceived of as "a chaos, a cauldron full of seething excitation." He wrote that the id "has no organization, produces no collective will, but only a striving to bring about the satisfaction of the instinctual needs subject to the observance of the pleasure principle." "The id of course knows

[30] *Ibid.*, p. 137. Parens and Saul state that Freud had already noted that functions which the parents carried out for the child were internalized in ego, including "patterns of reality testing, relating to objects, control and expression of instinctual drives, autonomous ego activity, defenses." *Dependence in Man*, p. 52.

[31] Schafer, "Ideals, Ego Ideal, and Ideal Self," pp. 139–40, 147.

no judgments of value: no good and evil, no morality. . . . Instinctual cathexes seeking discharge—that is all there is in the id."[32]

However, one can also find in Freud's writings passages which attribute a good deal of structure to the id.[33] Moreover, as we have stated, any number of psychoanalytic writers have more recently come to this same conclusion. Thus, "Even if we adopted the commonly held position within psychoanalysis that all the id can do is wish, mental content would not be excluded from the id. The very concept *wish* implies a representation of an object, an action, and a consummation." Further, "The relative weight of sexual and aggressive drives, and the relative emphasis on oral, anal, or phallic modes and zones of instinctual expression and satisfaction, bear the imprint of identification with parental models."[34] Among other things, this means not only that instinctual drives influence ego, but that ego in turn influences and patterns instinctual drives.[35] Social structure

---

[32] See R. R. Holt, "The Development of Primary Process: A Structural View," in *Motives and Thought*, ed. Holt, p. 361.

[33] *Ibid.*, pp. 362, 351–52, 356, 358.

[34] Schafer, "Ideals, Ego Ideal, and Ideal Self," *ibid.*, pp. 147, 140. In addition to Schafer and Holt (cited in the notes above), see also George S. Klein, "Peremptory Ideation," *ibid.*, pp. 84, 87, 106, 121–22; Merton Gill, "The Primary Process," *ibid.*, pp. 280, 287–88, 293, 296–97; Peter Wolff, "Cognitive Considerations for a Psychoanalytic Theory of Language Acquisition," *ibid.*, pp. 313–14; Schafer, *Aspects of Internalization*, pp. 148–49. Both Schafer and Holt cite Merton Gill, *Topography and Systems in Psychoanalytic Theory*, Psychological Issues, no. 10 (New York, 1963); and Schafer cites Max Schur, *The Id and the Regulatory Principles of Mental Functioning in Psychoanalysis* (New York, 1966); David Rapaport, *The Structure of Psychoanalytic Theory*, Psychological Issues, no. 6 (New York, 1960), pp. 60–65; K. M. Colby, *Energy and Structure in Psychoanalysis* (New York, 1955); Rafael Moses, "Form and Content," *Psychoanal. Stud. Child*, 23 (1968): 210–12; P. Noy, "A Revision of the Psychoanalytic Theory of the Primary Process," *Int. J. Psychoanal.*, 50, pt. 2 (1969): 155–77, esp. 158; Fred Pine, "On the Structuralization of Drive-Defense Relationships," *Psychoanal. Quart.*, 39, no. 1 (1970): 21; Douglas W. Orr, "Anthropological and Historical Notes on the Female Sexual Role," *J. Amer. Psychoanal. Ass.*, 16, no. 3 (July, 1968): 603; Anne Hayman, "What Do We Mean by 'Id,' " *ibid.*, 17, no. 2 (April, 1969): 353–80; Jacob A. Arlow, "Unconscious Fantasy and Disturbances of Conscious Experience," *Psychoanal. Quart.*, 38, no. 1 (1969): 4, 6, 8; Joseph T. Coltrera, "On the Creation of Beauty and Thought: The Unique as Vicissitude," *J. Amer. Psychoanal. Ass.*, 13, no. 3 (July, 1965): 659; Hans W. Loewald, "Psychoanalytic Theory and the Psychoanalytic Process," *Psychoanal. Stud. Child*, 25 (1970): 58. For stronger views on this issue, see "The Concept of the Id," reported by E. Marcovitz in *J. Amer. Psychoanal. Ass.*, 11, no. 1 (January, 1963): 51–53; and I. P. Glauber, "Federn's Annotation of Freud's Theory of Anxiety," *ibid.*, p. 91. See also p. 21 and nn. 35 and 36 of this volume.

[35] This point was made, e.g., by R. M. Loewenstein, "Conflict and Autonomous Ego Development during the Phallic Phase," *Psychoanal. Stud. Child*, 5(1950): 52. See also, e.g., John Halverson, "Amour and Eros in the Middle Ages," *Psychoanal. Rev.*, 57, no. 2 (1970): 253.

and interaction affect the individual down to the level of wish and fantasy.[36]

We may thus conclude that socialization occurs at all levels of the personality and that the consequent thoughts and behaviors are linked to the common culture. There are no actions which do not have *social* significance, and there are no thoughts which are not to some recognizable degree structured by particular historical and social circumstances. Both conscious *and* unconscious activities are influenced by the standards which prevail in particular times and places.

In sociological terms this means that, given the appropriate social structural conditions and historical circumstances, previously repressed wishes and fantasies can become conscious, and, *refined in the light of real conditions*, can provide the basis for action. At the conscious level these wishes codified as ideology will serve as explanation, justification, rationalization, and legitimation for whatever action becomes necessary. In this way such wishes and fantasies themselves become systematically routinized as conscious modes of expression, serving to take the place of previously internalized patterns. This results in new modes of achieving consensus, in concerted action on this basis, and particularly in action which is directed against institutionalized standards.

This does not mean that any or every aspect of unconscious thought can become conscious or that even some aspects which become conscious and are brought under control are experienced without conflict. The consequent critical analysis of authority or morality, for example, is never easily undertaken, nor is the possibility for conscious appraisal effective for everyone in the community. Moreover, there is no reason to expect that

[36] Holt has written that, "from the beginning of his life, a child is also exposed to culture, and to a special child's subculture, which contains numerous crystallized and far-reachingly organized primary process systems. Myths, legends, fairy stories, and other simple types of fiction incorporating recognizable forms of the primary process seem to be the favorite fare of young children in other societies besides our own. Despite their casual sadism and the terrifying archetypes that people them, these magical tales offer a comfortingly oversimplified view of a world that is within a child's grasp. I find it a fascinating possibility that they also comprise an indoctrination into consolidated and extended forms of the primary process, a cultural transmission of ways to dream, to fantasy consciously and unconsciously, even to construct delusional systems and other kinds of symptoms, ways that are culturally viable because rooted in certain kinds of world views." Holt, "The Development of Primary Process," pp. 374–75. See also George Devereaux, "Normal and Abnormal: The Key Concepts of Ethnopsychiatry," in *Man and His Culture: Psychoanalytic Anthropolgy after "Totem and Taboo*," ed. W. Muensterberger (London, 1969), pp. 113–36; and, for an opposing view, see Geza Roheim, "Dream Analysis and Field Work in Anthropology," *ibid.*, pp. 141–42.

the conscious appraisal of morality will produce a unilateral response, even among those who are aware of strain in some particular area. It is more likely that different communities of response will arise with regard to the social-historical issues at hand, creating an array of subgroups of opinion, ranging from those who are contemptuously critical and aggressive to those who actively support the extant morality without being consciously aware of the basis of their support.

These comments are crucial, and their implications must be made explicit. Ideologies (codified wishes and fantasies) as systematic bases for action which legitimate different or novel forms of behavior are not simply the product of instinctual drives, nor are they merely expressions of these drives. It may be argued that ideologies gratify unconscious wishes, and it is usually possible to identify a variety of drive contents in them. But this is an acceptable position only insofar as ego and reality functions are included and any implied notion of "endogenous potentiality" is not limited to drive expression; and only insofar as we understand that such unconscious wishes or drive manifestations are structured to some degree *from the beginning* by words, behaviors, feelings, and ideas immediately available in the environment, though not necessarily sanctioned by the moral order in which they appear. That is, the content ultimately expressed must have already acquired some structured form via identification with figures present in the external world.

Thus, individuals can cathect an idea (or an aspect of self or a form of behavior) only if they are in a position to inhibit any excessive anxiety that may result.[37] The general, systematic acceptance of an idea or form of behavior throughout a population requires that anxiety be constrained *on the basis of a common apprehension of a real problem* (no matter how regressively this may be interpreted and dealt with) and an attachment to ideology and leadership. Indeed, historically this has often required the intervention of a powerful authority figure. But, on the one hand, this is not necessarily a regressive feature of change, as we shall explain more fully later. And, on the other hand, we are now able to explain how such a leader is able to make his authority effective, or, rather, the basis on which his ideas and activities may inspire similar behavior in a mass of followers.

It is in these terms that we emphasize the notion that id impulses are channeled through, and expressed in, culturally definable and sanction-

[37] Seymour L. Lustman, "The Economic Point of View and Defense," *Psychoanal. Stud. Child,* 23 (1968): 199. Joseph Weiss, "The Emergence of New Themes: A Contribution to the Psychoanalytic Theory of Therapy," *Int. J. Psychoanal.,* 52 (1971): 459; Jules Weiss, "Continuing Research: The Modification of Defenses in Psychoanalysis," *J. Amer. Psychoanal. Ass.,* 20, no. 1 (January, 1972): 177–78.

able terms, or that these impulses, or the thoughts associated with them, can become conscious and can be brought under control. There are a variety of possible conditions under which this may occur. That is,

> an unconscious fantasy is invoked under conditions of a *current* threat, as, for instance, to self-esteem: (a) when a person finds himself in a realistic situation corresponding to the earlier traumatic experience; (b) when the realistic situation confronting him, while not traumatic, contains elements conforming to those of the unconscious fantasy, thus stimulating it; or (c) when he is subjected to stressful circumstances which bring about a change in state of consciousness that makes it possible for otherwise effectively segregated aspects of the fantasy to impose themselves upon behavior.[38]

But in all these (and in many more sociologically possible) conditions the effects of culture on all levels of personality will be manifest.

Once the problems of order and change are viewed in these psychosocial terms, explanations of group and mass behavior are possible. Patterns of behavior derived from the values and norms of particular social structures, including specifically economic and political institutions and practices, are transmitted through the family and then subsequently through other institutional agents of socialization. As individuals develop (in the sense intended by Erikson in his notion of "life cycle") they take on tasks and seek to fulfill aspirations in areas independent of the family; different social functions such as work (mastery) become crucial for identity, self-esteem, and narcissistic well-being. Because psychic (and hence social) stability is tied to political, economic, religious, and other functions, attachments to these must be examined in their own terms, from the standpoint of the reality factors involved, but also from the standpoint of sources of community and group support, fears of loss, wishes for greater or lesser separation from objects, and the like. It is necessary to keep in mind that moral mandates are internalized in superego but that standards for achievement and mastery are internalized in ego, and ego also thereby maintains standards for drive gratification, for the fulfillment of id wishes. Thus, ties to economic, political, religious, educational, and familial institutions represent so many situations of

---

[38] Klein, "Peremptory Ideation," p. 122; see also pp. 84, 87. Klein writes: "With its arousal, such a fantasy is motivational; it includes directives of approach and avoidance, of goal relevance and irrelevance, of behavioral selectivity generally. . . . There ensues a search for behavioral and perceptual equivalents that will repair the instigating conditions of experienced threat. In this sense, *unconscious fantasies are symbol-inducing motivations in their behavioral consequences.* Symbolism would be of the nature of environment-made-relevant to the particularizing tendencies of components of the fantasy, including wish and defense."

psychic stability or of potential instability. The normatively perceived failure of these institutions—of any one, or of a group of them, whether it be political or religious morality, or modes of production—leads to the inability of groups of people to combine internalized standards with other aspects of social life in order to produce "familiar actions." Personality is therefore affected at all levels, and, at the same time, groups are affected in a rather systematic way.

Clearly, identity has external as well as internal reference points. Identity is cathected with narcissistic libido, and narcissistic gratification is a legitimate gain from the exercise of character traits that develop within specific social environments. The inability to act in terms of social mandates that define and give structure to identity is therefore a narcissistic blow which threatens the integrity of identity and damages self-esteem. Such a condition interferes with the ways at one's disposal to live up to one's self-image.[39] Identity and esteem are therefore ultimately tied to societal membership (i.e., to status within groups and institutions) and hence to the external world.

For this reason, radical critics can refer to a given social structure as dangerous, exploitative, repressive, or irrelevant—and avoid lapsing into depression or apathetic withdrawal—only after they have organized an alternative morality and other standards for action. Radical activists will come into conflict with society, of course, because others do not share with them the new standards and expectations. But such individuals can, to a degree, maintain their new identity because it is ego syntonic and is supported by others around them. In this way the anxiety engendered by attacks on society is brought under control and positive action can be taken. Without both levels of support—that is, self and society—the radical critic is bound to experience chronic anxiety, a situation which leads inevitably to inaction.[40]

It may be argued that, once the Oedipus complex is resolved, the major source of self-esteem, or the primary judge of the moral appropriateness of aspects of identity, is superego. The shift that accompanies the oedipal resolution implies movement from a world of objects to a world of symbols;

[39] Blos, "Character Formation in Adolescence," pp. 246–57; Schafer, "Ideals, Ego Ideal, and Ideal Self," pp. 146–58; Joseph Sandler *et al.*, "The Ego Ideal and the Ideal Self," *Psychoanal. Stud. Child*, 18 (1963): 149; Joseph Sandler, "On the Concept of Superego," *ibid.*, 15 (1960): and Edward Bibring, "The Mechanism of Depression," in *Affective Disorders*, ed. Phyllis Greenacre (New York, 1953), pp. 24, 37–39. In Jacobson's terms the damage to self-esteem, the emotional expression of self-evaluation, represents the degree of discrepancy or harmony between the self-representations and the wished for concept of self. Edith Jacobson, *The Self and the Object World* (New York, 1964), p. 131.

[40] Parens and Saul, *Dependence in Man*, p. 131.

the oedipal transition separates aggressive and erotic tendencies from basic drives and from original objects so that one can act on abstract standards and expectations (i.e., "secondary autonomy"). However, for individuals and groups the ability to act systematically on these abstract standards depends not so much on the family, or on internalized mental representations of familial objects, as it does on the wider social and cultural world remaining relatively available and "predictable" so that ego and superego structures continue to be effective.[41] Some reliable and consistent interpretation of this background is always necessary.

It is in this context that the importance of the wider social world should be stressed and the role of the family and of the unique individual integrated in a more balanced way. Of course, early socialization is a crucial aspect of the problem. But personality is not a static entity, and, as ego and superego develop, so too do needs and ambitions, and areas of activity evolve and expand. It is a mistake to think that individuals derive gratification from, or strive to please, only familial objects, or that they view themselves as enhanced or diminished only in reference to such objects, or that their internal integrity derives only from the strength of these early internalizations. It is, after all, society that determines that certain valued "reality areas" will become especially important in the development of individuals. This is accomplished initially through the family; that is, in a temporal sense, the way an individual initially adapts to

---

[41] Roy Schafer, "The Loving and Beloved Superego in Freud's Structural Theory," *Psychoanal. Stud. Child*, 15 (1960): 163; *idem*, "Ideals, Ego Ideal, and Ideal Self," p. 169; Sandler, "On the Concept of Superego," *Psychoanal. Stud. Child*, p. 157. The oedipal transition allows the individual to dispense with erotic rewards as the primary mechanism of socialization, which is henceforth based on internalized values, images, ideals, etc. In our sense, then, we can say that self-esteem is dependent upon, and cannot be supported or elevated in the absence of, a functioning social structure, no matter how independent one is of his family—that is, authority structures and ideals at the social and cultural level and a sense of "executive" capacity and standards for drive and ego activity at the personal level. On self-esteem the following should also be noted: "Alfred Adler has taken one source of lowered self-esteem (organ inferiority) and embroidered it into a whole system. And although we reject Adler's highly oversimplified views, the techniques by which the ego can restore its self-esteem and the ways in which these techniques enter into character have been insufficiently studied." *Ibid.*, p. 157. See also Otto Fenichel, "Depression and Mania," in *The Meaning of Despair*, ed. W. Gaylin (New York, 1968), p. 139. On secondary autonomy, see Erik Erikson, *Identity and the Life Cycle*, Psychological Issues, no. 1 (New York, 1959), pp. 15–16. Erikson indicates that the variety of modes of behavior (inceptive, retentive, intrusive) can become separated from their origins and achieve a level of autonomous functioning. Secondary autonomy means that the erotic and destructive trends involved in psychic functioning are at a distance from basic drives; they "exist in forms, probably relatively securely fused, that contribute to adaptive superego functioning rather than to the archaic, exhibitionistic, and instinct loaded manifestations of guilt as are found in the obsessional neurosis and melancholia."

any reality area will be shaped by the way his parents deal with it.[42] But, as the child's ego and superego expand and differentiate, and as he incorporates the social mandates of teachers and friends, as well as those of other collectivities and institutions, the effects of familial objects become less direct because they are combined with a number of other orientations to, and levels of, social life.

The individual may thus achieve a measure of independence from familial objects, but he remains attached to the wider society, and he can act as long as social and cultural environments remain to some degree intact. The failure of political, economic, or, for that matter, familial structures threatens personal and group identity, and the resulting conflict must be resolved at the appropriate level; and it can be resolved in a relatively autonomous way.

No matter how stably superego mandates have been internalized, no matter how smooth the resolution of oedipal conflict has been, no matter how independent of familial objects one has become, neither personal identity nor the capacity to maintain it is ever that independent of the wider environment. Political, economic, religious, and other structures (including, of course, the family) comprise a background against which people act, and such action promises to be viable only as long as the patterns of behavior remain legitimate and/or available. Internalizations are stabilizing and are the source of rewards only as long as the *social* world holds together. The real, effective presence of external agencies and their reliability, or the reliability of standards and expectations symbolized in external objects, is the condition for adequate observation of self and others, and for activity which can allow the approximation of actual self to ideal self. The failure of cultural and social symbols and mandates, a failure which violates, contradicts, or renders ineffective or disappointing internalizations at all levels of the personality, constitutes the primary source of radical demands against the environment and leads to the reformation of identity.

On the one hand, therefore, it can be stated that all men are vulnerable and exposed with regard to their attachments to society. This is one important reason for idealization and exaggeration of the virtues of leaders, states, nations, moralities, and the like. Freud explained man's clinging to a belief in the existence of a protective God-father because this figure is more powerful than he discovered his real father to be. But this kind of idealization is also directed toward political authority, the state, ideology, culture, the historical past—in brief, to a variety of activities "out there"

[42] Douglas Holmes, "A Contribution to a Psychoanalytic Theory of Work," *Psychoanal. Stud. Child*, 21 (1966): 388–89, 386.

which must appear grander than they are. Disruptions of society are therefore not easily tolerated, and men will fight either to preserve the traditional symbolic codes that have regulated their lives or to establish new codes. One thing we can say with certainty: men cannot act, and will not live, in the absence of such symbolic codes.

At the same time that society appears to people to be somewhat larger than life, at least in the sense that the symbolic codes which bind society are not so easily questioned and are always somewhat removed from the possibility of critical analysis, society also provides the basis for realistic activities—that is, for activities which are not oriented to familial objects or gratifications. It has been suggested that no one can be fully integrated into group life until libido has been transferred from parents to the self (e.g., has become manifest as ego interests) and to the community. But this means that the community, in whatever form, is independent of, and represents something other than, the family. The development of superego—strictly a social function—facilitates the desexualization of activity and prevents the restoration of original, primal relationships. The paramount role of society is to support and sustain activity at the level of abstract standards and expectations and to avoid regressive behavior—except within explicit boundaries, as in sexual behavior, play, and ritual. The importance of society in this respect is never so evident as when it fails.

On the other hand, social and psychic functions are not fixed. Novel situations occur, new social demands are made, and ego can be organized to cope with these demands; men can organize themselves for new and different tasks.

> The role that the process of adaptation . . . plays in this must not be underestimated. . . . [W]e are constantly confronted with new problems as we go along in the solution of old ones. Moreover, man is capable of modifying his environment, and these modifications frequently carry with them the need to adapt to new changed conditions and the solution of sometimes new and unsuspected problems. The modifications I have in mind here refer not only to the physical conditions of his milieu and their multiple derivations but to those in our social, political, philosophical, and even religious systems.[43]

---

[43] Nagera, "The Concepts of Structure and Structuralization," p. 98. "The development of ego interests calls away from the love object not only part of the libido but also part of the aggression which . . . can become vested in new personal and inanimate objects." Jacobson, *The Self and the Object World*, p. 78. See also Schafer, *Aspects of Internalization*, p. 30; Parsons, *Social Structure and Personality*, chaps. 1–4 and 8 (pp. 17–111 and 183–235); H. Hartmann, E. Kris and R. M. Loewenstein, "Culture and Personality," *Papers*, pp. 103–4, 109.

Freud assumed that society exercises control over individuals because morality is internalized in superego, and that, because political authority is a representation of familial authority, the cost of transgression would be too high. But, to the extent that this is true, society, and especially its coercive apparatus, would appear to be superfluous. Freud thought further, then, that society must retain an effective priority because men resent the demands for renunciation of instinctual gratification made and enforced by society, and, in spite of the binding power of the internalized morality, the "return of the repressed" is always possible. Men will seek to gratify oedipal wishes. In Freud's view men long to rebel, and, when we see instances of rebellion, these stand as proof of an internal instinctual dynamic, motivating behavior. But, whatever value one wants to put on it, the fact is that men are for the most part compliant, they tolerate even oppressive social orders, and would continue to do so if the external world remained stable—that is, if it continued to be possible to act on internalized standards and expectations. Thus, the normatively perceived failure, or the threatened failure of a society, and not the resentment of its prohibitions or impositions, determines mass action at the social level. People are driven to rebellion not out of the frustrations imposed by group living as such, but out of the aggression that is generated when mandates are violated or cannot be acted upon. Personal and group identity and the capacity to maintain it is at issue, not the extent of renunciation of instinctual fulfillment.

What we may conclude from the foregoing remarks is that individuals cannot act at will on impulse or on the basis of conscious, calculated aspirations. Society could never maintain an adequate level of order on such bases. On the other hand, their behavior is not wholly determined by unconscious processes either. Rather, autonomous activity can be organized, and novel modes of behavior can follow from the response to the objective failures of society. People can and do respond realistically to the circumstances that affect them. This does not preclude an idiosyncratic level of response, and at no point do we exclude the possibility of regressive and/or destructive forms of response. But a formulation of the concepts of identity, character, and social structure which accounts for personal and social achievements in the terms offered here is more consistent with the empirical data than are the traditional psychoanalytic approaches.

By raising the level of abstraction, we can integrate the remarks we have made pertaining both to identity and to the structured quality of id processes. Basically what is being proposed is a "cybernetic" model in which inputs to action from "higher" and "lower" orders of phenomena combine, but in which the main focus of control of action patterning resides in symbol systems. The inputs to action which are combined include information (a higher order) and energy (a lower order). In social and personality systems, energy is derived from the behavioral organism, and information is derived from cultural meanings and symbols.[44]

At the genetic level, the organism is relatively immune from symbolic influence or control. However, within the organism, endogenous affective or cognitive potentialities are influenced by symbol learning, and therefore are open to control from the higher-order levels of human action systems. In these terms, personality and society stand between the organism and the cultural system. Personality and social systems both function to integrate and organize energy and information. In personality, the integration of the underlying organic system is achieved by linking it to informational sources through the socialization process. Thus, the familiar components of personality—motivational sources (id), reality orientations (ego), personal conscience (superego), and also identity—are linked to the organic and symbolic levels.[45]

At the organic level—or, in psychological terms, at the level of the id—certain elements are not amenable to symbolic control; but the better part of human action which expresses this level is open to such control, whether the action is directly expressed (as erotic and aggressive impulses causing personal and social disruption) or is manifest in a socialized way (e.g., as "normal" sexual activity, work, etc.). Symbol systems penetrate deeply and facilitate the integration of motivational sources so that expression for the most part occurs in a legitimated context.

At the same time, and at the other end of the scale, identity brings together within the personality all of the internalized patterns derived from these different sources. Identity refers to the organization of patterns of behavior (the basis for the expression of an extraordinary variety of contents) which enable the individual to deal with, and adapt to, ongoing and conflictual internal and external situations. Once identity is organized, changes in patterns (i.e., radical change, as opposed to changes in specific contents) are resisted and are in any case extremely affecting. As identity means the coordination of every level of the personality, radical change means alteration at every level of the personality. Thus, not only

[44] This is derived from Talcott Parsons, "General Introduction II: An Outline of the Social System," in Talcott Parsons, Edward Shils, Kasper D. Naegele, and Jesse R. Pitts, *Theories of Society: Foundations of Modern Sociological Theory*, 2 vols. (Glencoe, Ill., 1961), pp. 30–79; and from Talcott Parsons, personal communication; Bellah, *Beyond Belief*; and A. Hunter Dupree, "A System of Biological, Social, Cultural, and Physical Systems," unpublished paper.

[45] On identity as a "fourth structure," see e.g., Anne Hayman, "Verbalization and Identity," *Int. J. Psychoanal.*, 46 (October, 1965).

is the violation of morality a problem (superego transgression), but the individual's very practical skills, his ordinary daily mode of control over the environment is threatened (transgression of ego standards). This is why radical demands for change arouse so much passion, for or against, and why charismatic leaders are able to organize a mass following in revolutionary situations.

There is, of course, the problem of the unique personality and of idiosyncratic forms of behavior. But there is also the problem of social order; this problem at the theoretical level must therefore be solved in such a way as to account for the reality of individual variations. The most important aspect of this theoretical resolution is the symbolic system, the broad framework within which societies and personalities are organized and integrated. This symbolic system offers meaning to social and personal action systems and it also motivates and directs behavior. The symbol system may be variegated, but in spite of this diversity it is also integrated and finite, in the sense that there is some relationship between and among all the cultural symbols, and the limits of expression are recognizable to members of the society. On the basis of such organizational mandates it is possible to conceive of a great variety of personal behaviors, but also, at the same time, of a coherent social system.

This symbolic code, which is more specific and institutionalized at the social level, constitutes the standard for appropriate patterns of action for groups. In the individual, these symbols are internalized as appropriate standards for personal behavior. At both levels, the organization of the symbolic code can be variant. There is never a perfect relationship between the two levels, and it is always necessary for individuals to "work out" in action what these relationships are; this includes a continuous effort to see that the code is implemented. Situations of conflict which stem from social-structural conditions beyond anyone's ability to control, as well as deviant occurrences, provide the problems for adjustment.

It should be clear that we are not treating individuals and groups as if they are responding to "real" objects—although these must lie behind any human system. Rather, what is at issue are internalized standards and expectations. Failure, disappointment, abandonment, or the threat of these possibilities is important only insofar as such a normatively perceived violation impinges upon a symbolic standard.[46] In these terms persons

[46] Kenneth Gaarder, "The Internalized Representation of the Object," *ibid.*, 46 (July, 1965): 297. Codes may fail in their function as directives. In spite of the elasticity and the latitude of permitted interpretation of symbolic codes, the real situational circumstances may not be feasibly integrated by the extant codes. In such circumstances more general, or even new, codes develop.

and groups are oriented to the symbolic code, and failure on this level is threatening and decisive for action. It is in these terms that Durkheim's notion of society having a reality *sui generis* should be understood.

Thus, the priority of cultural and social systems is explicit, and this is theoretically both necessary and advantageous. Reductionist biological frameworks cannot explain change or variation in human patterning. Reductionist psychological explanations cannot make intelligible the relationship of human individuality to the social order. In a similar way, theory that stresses particular object relationships cannot adequately explain concerted or collective action; each individual in this context must appear as the idiosyncratic product of his private experience. Furthermore, theories that emphasize one institutional reality—the economy, the family, or the political order—by the same token reduce all responses and variation in action in the differing realms to reflections of action in the assumedly more fundamental realm; indeed, such theory cannot comprehend personal and societal variation as a possible human condition. The symbolic control of action systems, however, brings together the several levels of analysis without reducing or otherwise violating any of them.

Although there is more to be said along these lines, one important point that should be stressed is the fundamental articulation between personality and society as action systems which stems from the "unconscious" commitment in both systems to the same set of generalized symbolic codes. There is in this frame of reference no necessarily irreconcilable antipathy between the individual and society—although we can see why demands for radical change would arise. This avoids, at the same time, reductionist views, which either collapse society to the individual (i.e., which view social objects as functions of projection, wish fulfillment, collective defense, etc.) or treat the individual as a mere epiphenomenon of social order (i.e., there are variations which stem from genetic make-up, from constitutional endowment, and from the varying perceptions of objects which derive from such differences, accounting for unique, discrete personalities). Thus, both society and individual are conceived of as somewhat interdependent action systems.[47]

[47] Philip E. Slater, *Microcosm: Structural, Psychological, and Religious Evolution in Groups* (New York, 1966).

Needless to say, the only issue involved here is whether psychoanalytic insight can be accommodated to historical and sociological data, and whether the more sociological approach is consistent with known facts. Other writers, of course, have attempted to organize an approach that includes social-structural factors as independent variables. They have been criticized in turn by the adherents of the traditional views, particularly from this point of view: "One of the crucial commonalities in the thought of Horney, Fromm, Sullivan, Kardiner, *et al.*, is that psychological turmoil and discontent within people is a function of the social institutions in which they are raised and through which they seek fulfillment. Yet their insistence on the causal efficacy of culture—that is on culture as a separate reality confronting individuals— . . . verges on declaring a radical separation between the individual and society." Whatever the problems with these earlier writers, and they are many, we have not postulated any radical separation between personality and culture. At the same time, it is hard to take Freud's notion of superego seriously (i.e., that the child internalizes his father's morality) and not view society in some sense as an independent reality, capable of being analyzed in those terms; it is equally hard not to amplify what Freud could have meant with regard to ego development in terms of identification, internalization, and object relations. Part of the problem here has to do with origins—that is, "some purposive and intentional processes of the human organism must be identified that exist *before culture* and which transact with experience to produce and maintain culture." In phylogenetic terms we do not know what existed before culture, and neither does anyone else. But, if we had to guess what prompted such complex organization, we would choose anxiety, not only or necessarily in terms of superego and castration, but also in terms of the feared loss of loved objects and the love of those objects; moreover, we would stress fears of external as well as internal reality, fears of the loss of control over reality (ego dissolution), and the need to master reality in terms of food, shelter, defense, etc. In ontogenetic terms, there may be endogenous potentialities, but these are selectively structured by "caretaking" figures—that is, are given form in terms of the values and mandates of the society into which one is born. Undoubtedly there are idiosyncratic features, and these may be of interest in biographical studies. But there are also systematic sociological features, which, for historical purposes, are more important. The quoted material is from B. J. Bergen and S. D. Rosenberg, "The New Neo-Freudians: Psychoanalytic Dimensions of Social Change," *Psychiatry*, 34, no. 1 (1971): 24.

V. On Social Stability and Social Change

The recasting of psychoanalytic propositions in psychosocial terms allows us to pursue a rather novel kind of historical and social analysis. What we can now undertake to examine is affective behavior—a generic category which refers to obligated types of emotional expression between and among individuals and groups—at the *social* level. Our special focus, in other words, is on affective exchange as a social component in interaction between individuals as members of groups or institutions. The underlying assumptions in social, as in individual, terms are: that every relationship has an emotional component; that conscious and unconscious, positive and negative, feelings are invested in self and others; and that, although at any given time these emotional components are internalized (on the psychic side) and institutionalized (in roles, on the social side), they are also subject to change.

In the sociological sense, affect is one basis for integrating individuals into social organization. It is particularly the basis for "telling" individuals that they are being rewarded or sanctioned, that they are members in good standing or bad, that their actions are consonant with their social identity, and so on. Certainly idiosyncratic feelings are expressed in any social situation. But shared feelings also are expressed, and account for social coordination and the subjective experience of acting appropriately in terms of self and others. Social change refers, of course, to change in the ways of systematically evaluating and categorizing persons, social statuses, and roles. But, at the same time, this also refers to systematic change in group feelings.

There are, then, four levels of social process which can be examined in this context: the legitimate and sanctioned expressions of emotion which tend to stabilize social interaction; the conditions under which these expressions are disrupted and become inappropriate, dysfunctional, or destructive; the various possible reactions to changed relationships that result from such disruption; and the conditions under which stabilized behavior and emotional expression can be re-established. Because of the differences that derive from the varied circumstances of time and place, we cannot in an a priori fashion suggest what will be done concerning any or all of these dimensions in prospective situations. But we can say to an important degree what *was* done in the past.[1]

It is, of course, impossible to distinguish and to elaborate upon here all of the ramifications implied in this use of psychoanalytic constructs, or the full range of problems which such constructs can help to clarify. Considering the conceptual and terminological breadth of the theory, and the problems involved in relating the theory to other disciplines and to different types of data, all we can effectively do is suggest some of the possibilities and point out some of the pitfalls involved in employing psychoanalytic concepts.

To begin with, there are two fundamental aspects of the concept of object relationships around which the psychosocial investigation of obligated patterns of expression can conveniently be organized. One is comprised of internalization and identification processes, the basic means by which situations of stability are organized; the other involves the notion of object loss, the normatively perceived passing or failure of, disappointment in, abandonment or betrayal by loved or otherwise valued persons, institutions, symbols, and even aspects of self. Internalization, identification, and object loss are obviously deductively linked to each other and linked in turn to such paired objects of study as the individual and the group, and external and internal reality. This general framework provides the essential theoretical foundation for an examination of the most basic concerns of history and sociology, the problems of order and change.

We have referred to internalization at various points above, but now we can deal with it in more consistent sociological terms. We have already suggested that man's behavior in society is organized and to a significant degree is bound by obligated and patterned expressions of emotion. A number of formal and informal symbolic codes both account for the pattern and connect these emotional ties with intellectual processes and institutional organizations. Included in these are religious and moral codes and a variety of expressive and cognitive symbols, and, at other levels (distinguishing here between values and norms), there are legal, political, economic, familial, and educational symbolic standards.

---

[1] We do not think it important that we are suggesting that this frame of reference is only postdictive. It is important, however, that we are suggesting that there are no universal actions and affectual responses. This proposition precludes prediction. Further, this proposition separates our work from all other psychohistorical approaches. The advantage of this position is that it brings our analytic statements closer to historical and sociological reality and, to a degree, obviates the glossing of history with theoretical categories.

These ties are also given form in the way that people behave toward each other. Individuals are socialized through the transmission of ways to act and react, a process which is initiated by, but is by no means limited to, the earliest relationship of parents, especially the mother, to children. The individual is oriented to action in *his* society by the internalization of values as the values are given symbolic meaning in the patterns of interaction which affect the individual and others in his environment. Internalization may be taken to mean that values or patterns of behavior are not, under most circumstances, extensively or to a significant degree consciously attended to or available for manipulation or critical and facile examination and repudiation.

Social stability may then be understood to derive from the acceptance of a common culture—in brief, from the acceptance of a "commonly shared system of symbols, the meanings of which are understood on both sides with an approximation to agreement." This system of shared symbols provides the background for concerted and organized behavior, for the orientation to, and interpretation and evaluation of, courses of action, and for the definition of self and others. To an important extent, then, order is a result of the shared meanings and of the emotionally founded obligation to adhere to these as the basis for the interpretation of action and feelings.

We may infer from this that the highest order of phenomena in any society is the value system. The internalization of the value system represents an effective control over behavior on one level because moral rules then constrain behavior "most fundamentally by moral authority rather than by external coercion."[2] On another level, ego standards for achievement and for the gratification of wishes are also constrained by definitions of legitimate behavior. The ways in which individuals and groups manifest skill or seek success may be diverse, but they are limited, particularly by unreflected commitments to given definitions of what is appropriate behavior. Of course, in both random and systematic ways the common culture is being transgressed all the time. People interpret codes

[2] The quotes are from Talcott Parsons, *Social Structure and Personality* (Glencoe, Ill., 1964), pp. 21, 19. This may raise some questions as to an "idealist" interpretation of social process. It must be said, then, that values and symbolic codes are a part of history, social structure, and personal identity and that they derive from objective relationships on both institutional and personal levels. They are rooted in social conditions on one side (including modes of production) and in somatic processes on the other. The point is that there must be some profound relationship between personality and social structure which can be identified as determinative of the types of behavior we are considering—that is, systematic behavior of the widest range, from communal cooperation to destructive rage. We conceive of this point of contact as internalized symbolic codes. In this sense the question of idealist versus materialist is a false one.

in the light of situational and temporal exigencies, and variations in the expected patterns occur. Most structural variations, however, are understood to be rather routine and are easily justified. They thus go unnoticed or are not assessed as violations of the code. Some actions, however, are understood as violations, and there are social standards for the assessment of such actions as illegitimate (characterized, e.g., as criminal behavior or mental illness); in addition, a number of techniques are employed by other individuals and social agencies to enforce compliance. In obvious ways these techniques range from gifts and direct rewards to the outright use of force and coercion.

However, force or fear of external compulsion cannot be the overriding determinant of compliance. In a paradoxical sense the revolutionary is proof of this. The revolutionary decries the brutality of a society, its oppressive and exploitative features, and he justifies the withdrawal of his allegiance in these terms. Force cannot make him comply with the repudiated social mandates. The revolutionary has become emotionally committed and oriented to another course of action, whatever that may be. The revolutionary acts on different mandates, and threats of punishment are not deterrents.

Moreover, self or class interest (whether based on impulsive, spontaneous desires or on rational calculation) cannot be the sole determining factor of compliance either. Obviously, interest is a basis for action, but, if it were the only, or the decisive, basis, each individual (or group) could (and would) go off in his own direction any time it was useful for him to do so. The point is that this does not happen, and we know that values and norms will be attended to, even though they may run counter to rationality and interest.

Adherence to internalized norms is more readily enforced by techniques equivalent to that process—that is, by means which are not necessarily rational or conscious. One means of compliance (an index of the unconscious commitment to values) is the self-evaluative functions of personality, the psychological reactions to violation which, with maturation, become functions of stability (e.g., guilt, shame, anxiety, remorse, etc.). And, while under certain conditions and with certain individuals these evaluative functions may be circumvented, suppressed, or otherwise overcome, for the greatest number of people the greatest part of the time they are operative and thus serve generally to ensure stability.

Another means for achieving stability derives from the need to have the self defined continually by self and others. For example, membership in a group of any size is always a critical feature of self-definition and self-evaluation, and individuals are *always* striving in their actions to retain a definition of self as the member of a group. It is understood that persistent deviations will lead to segregation and isolation. Of course, it is relatively easy for individuals to move in and out of groups—as long as they remain stably connected somewhere. But isolation from *all* groups (as with solitary confinement) is certainly one of the harshest of human experiences. Thus, society is organized so that those who participate in it have been socialized to "know," share, and employ the common culture as the basis and background for concerted action. The social order is not chaotic for most people most of the time because of the common meanings that are unconsciously held and shared to some minimum degree.[3]

To be sure, internalization of the common culture cannot in itself be the total explanatory variable in the analysis of social stability. But it is a most important aspect of everyday life and must be if the subjective experience of order is to exist for individuals and groups. The continuous threatened or actual application of force to achieve compliance with dictates would lead ultimately to a sense of helplessness and to resignation and despair—or to interminable civil war—while the possibility of repudiating the common culture at will would make the social environment anomic at the subjective and objective levels—that is, in experiential and observational terms. For this reason, the transgression of internalized patterns of behavior—even if there is a realistic basis for such transgression—occurs only with great personal stress. And others who observe such transgression experience anxiety; continued transgression will be met by rigid, schematic, and violent responses because both the internal and external worlds are threatened by it.

In order to illustrate the usefulness of the internalization concept, let us take an extreme example. Historically there have been societies that included serfdom or slavery as a central institution. It is undeniable that repressive physical force was employed by those in control, and that force was an important means for achieving compliance with dictates. Still, we know that force has not always been a sufficient means for maintaining compliance; people have faced death in rebellion against oppressive conditions. The question, then, is how did societies that maintained

[3] We are not suggesting one reality for all members of a society, nor even one reality for all the members of a small group within a society. We mean, rather, that an approximation to shared meanings is used in action as the background for organizing behavior. The exact expression of symbolic codes must be worked out situationally, and this includes efforts to assure that within tolerable limits the codes are implemented. There is no single reality for individuals in a society; individual experience and perspective, movement from one social space to another, precludes that. But neither is there total individuality. Internalization and identification processes prevent this from occurring. Peter Berger and Thomas Luckmann, *The Social Construction of Reality* (New York, 1967).

serfdom or slavery over a relatively long period of time manage any level of stability or productivity? More generally, how can one explain stability and productive contribution in any instance in which significant elements of a population are systematically excluded from participation in decision-making processes and are expected and required to accept a dependent, passive, and subordinate position?

We would argue that this is typically derived from the compliance engendered in the internalization process. At one level this means the unconscious and (relatively) unreflected acceptance of passivity and subordination as legitimate; it implies an unconscious commitment to the rectitude and appropriateness of the principle of exclusion. At another level, internalization sets the parameters within which one defines oneself in relation to others. It is possible, of course, to point to any number of individual instances of achievement, or of personal and mass rebellion in societies organized in a rigidly hierarchical way. But the more general conclusion is that, historically, in the absence of a degree of destructiveness, or of a degree of the withdrawal of efficiency—or even of apathy—sufficient to render any system that enforced subordination insupportable, the assumption of internalized morality, with the consequences this has for order, is of explanatory value.[4]

It should be clear at this point that in a systematic way social structures can and do encourage autonomous and critical capacities among people —or they can strive to maintain grand images of inviolable and unassailable authority, discouraging reality testing, critical analysis of the environment, and other such ego functions. Society defines the possible courses of action open to people just as society is instrumental in the development

---

[4] As we have observed before, it is necessary to distinguish between idiosyncratic instances and forms of behavior which are or become systematically available, as exemplified in the development of ideology or in the institutionalization of a variety of practices. Moreover, a number of types of empirical instances are better accounted for in terms of internalization—for example, those situations in which badly disadvantaged groups have fought to preserve a morality and patterns of behavior which legitimated their exploitation and subordination. Very often, for example, peasant rebellions in Europe were launched to restore or retain traditional patterns of mastery and gratification which were interpreted as having been violated; these rebellions were not intended to implement a new morality, much less one that included, say, personal or group autonomy as a goal. Moreover, historically, there were instances of the withdrawal of emotion leading to apathy, as expressed, for example, in the incapacity to bear children. There are also instances of destructive behavior (rebellion) and examples of deliberate inefficiency (work slowdowns, etc.). This, however, does not contradict the essential point. What we want to suggest most specifically is that, considering the cruelty and oppressiveness of Russian serfdom or American slavery, these systems could not have been sustained at any level of productivity, and no degree of loyalty or substantial degree of order could have been maintained, unless the internalization process was to some degree effective.

of cognitive, affectual, and evaluative capacities. What must be considered as "normal" ego strength depends upon the identifications and internalizations provided by the caretaking and authoritative persons with whom the individual interacts; and the sense of self that one must live up to can include the need to be humble, submissive, and obedient.[5]

The use of the internalization concept should not be taken to imply a belief in the existence of, or possibility for, static social situations. As we explained earlier, every known society is differentiated to some degree, at least along the lines of age and sex. Any degree of differentiation implies the organization of ego and superego processes on the basis of which judgments can be made as to whether or not relevant mandates are being fairly implemented. The violation of certain mandates in any society is bound to lead to demands for the redress of grievances.[6] Moreover, no social order can ever implement the morality which undergirds it to a perfect degree. The disparity between the ideal representation of the values and the real extent to which this is effective—combined with a legitimated capacity to judge—leads continuously to action at the social level.[7]

No society, therefore, can ever be described as static. The question that is primarily raised by the internalization concept is why social change transpires within a given value structure in some instances but takes a revolutionary form (i.e., is aimed at the value structure) in other instances. In part, an answer to this question relates to the distinction made earlier between patterns and contents. Social change occurs within a value system when to a significant extent contents, and not patterns, are involved. Social change also occurs within a given system when some pattern of behavior is violated, but *not* as a result of a social-structural change which

[5] Up to the present time, for example, the female child has adapted to this society and to reality less by direct, immediate, critical contact than by the medium of close, loving relations to whom she has remained tied. See Roy Schafer, "Ideals, Ego Ideal, and Ideal Self," in *Motives and Thought: Essays in Honor of David Rapaport*, ed. R. R. Holt, Psychological Issues, no. 18/19 (New York, 1967), p. 169; Arnold H. Modell, *Object Love and Reality* (New York, 1968), pp. 54–88; Heinz Hartmann, "Notes on the Reality Principle," *Essays*, p. 258 n. 6; F. J. Hacker, "The Discriminatory Function of the Ego," *Int. J. Psychoanal.*, 43 (November–December, 1962): 401; Hernán Davanzo, "A Contribution to the Analysis of Resistance in Neurotic Dependence," *ibid.*, p. 442.

[6] Ego functions, for example, allow individuals to assess the fairness of their treatment in relation to their status (e.g., as citizens), or in relation to their relative contribution to the society (as with the demands made by workers in pluralized industrial societies), or in relation generally to the internalized standards and expectations of their society.

[7] It is necessary for personal stability that order be maintained. Individuals are willing to accept very wide ranges of expression, but they assert at the same time that the standards are still being maintained. But implicit in flexible standards are limits to the tolerance for ambiguity, and, when the limits are transgressed, action will follow.

has rendered this pattern ineffective or dysfunctional. In this case, violation is experienced primarily in superego terms, and this is not decisive for the emergence of radical forms of action. On the one hand, society can deal with this type of violation through legal and other types of sanctions, and, on the other hand, ego is not affected, in terms of either its standards for achievement or those for drive gratification. Thus, in this instance, the basis for stability still exists.

Social change also occurs within a value system as a function of the extent to which values are generalized and inclusive. That is, individuals and groups systematically excluded from participation in vital social processes can demand (and expect) change within a given system, to the extent that exclusion was based on standards and expectations not applicable to the general population. The fact that such exlcusion ultimately affects the ego ideal, ego standards for achievement and gratification, as well as superego, will force excluded groups to seek redress inasmuch as self-esteem, narcissistic integrity, and identity are involved. The discrepancies in access to the sources and symbols of power and prestige can become intolerable. In this case too, it should be noted, social-structural change is decisive in that the bases for emotional compliance with mandates for dependence and passivity must disappear before demands can be generalized and movements organized. To a great degree this results typically from the experience of inclusion on one level—particularly the economic or the educational level, because either implies the mastery of techniques useful to society—so that exclusion on other levels becomes onerous.

It is in these terms of the common culture that we can understand better the origins and goals of the contemporary civil rights and women's movements (which seek the inclusion in decision-making processes on virtually all institutional levels of particular groups of people hitherto excluded on ascriptive grounds), and the students' movement (which seeks inclusion for all people regardless of age, sex, or race on one institutional level hitherto closed to general participation). These movements are quite affecting, but for the most part they are well within the given standards and expectations of the society (i.e., autonomy and inclusion on the basis of merit and competence, and the termination of judgments on the basis of ascriptive criteria). In addition, these movements, especially with regard to the leadership, have a rather consistent class basis, a result primarily of the internalization and identification processes. It would not be difficult, in other words, to demonstrate the extensive participation of middle- and upper-class persons in the moderate and radical wings of these movements, or the capacity of working-class individuals and groups to support a narrower, less inclusive status quo, although in objective terms it is not particularly favorable to them.[8]

Revolutionary demands for change occur when standards and expectations are rendered ineffective or dysfunctional as a result of social-structural change. Personality is then affected on all levels, not only in terms of morality, but also in that the ego's capacity to master internal and external reality is disrupted. In this instance the basis for stability no longer exists and must be reorganized. Historically, one identifiable and recurrent response to this type of situation has been a demand for the restoration of traditional mandates and patterns of behavior. However, considering the type of social change we have in mind—for example, changes in the mode of agricultural production and distribution to accommodate the needs of a centralizing nation-state with its concomitant bureaucratic and urban organizations; or the types of change typically associated with the industrialization process—such a solution could not in the long run have proved satisfactory. If we consider the European state system only, the competition and rivalries between and among the powers for pride of place ensured that such a solution could not endure. Economically and politically no state could afford to repudiate the centralizing tendencies or the industrialization process. The more consistent conclusion has been for identity and life style to change. Hence, the difficulties in accepting these changes without disruption, without the intervention of charismatic leaders, without ideology, and so forth.

Identification with, and the internalization of, mandates and patterns of behavior of loved persons is the means by which character is initially organized. Identification serves the purpose of renunciation in the dissolution of the Oedipus complex. Identification is also the means of securing the love of important persons and of making oneself safe from attack (either from actual persons or from the internalized representations of persons). But identification also serves the function of mastery. This means, however, that personality is articulated to, and dependent upon, social modes, not only at all structural levels (superego, including ego ideal, ego, and id), but at all age levels as well.

[8] Aileen S. Kraditor, ed., *Up from the Pedestal: Selected Writings in the History of American Feminism* (Chicago, 1968), pp. 15ff.; Cary Cherniss, "Personality and Ideology: A Personological Study of Women's Liberation," *Psychiatry*, 35, no. 2 (May, 1972): 109–25, esp. 113–14. For a summary of the background of student activists, see S. M. Lipset, *Rebellion in the University* (Boston, 1971), chap. 3 ("Who Are the Activists"), pp. 80–123; and Robert Liebert, *Radical and Militant Youth* (New York, 1971), chap. 4 ("Who Were the Rebels?"), pp. 70–91. It should be noted that women, homosexuals, and others are seeking change in the evaluation of sexual symbols and, ultimately, changed identities.

At the level of superego and ego ideal,[9] mastery as a function of the identification process refers in the first place to the parents' mediating influence on primitive, archaic (preoedipal) ideals and prohibitions. Mandates acquire a realistic content in the socialization process as a result of the human contact provided by caretaking persons. The primitive apprehension of ideals (perfect and omnipotent) and of prohibitions (terrifying forms of punishment such as castration) cannot continue unmodified. What it is that one should strive to be and what it is that one must not do eventually come to be understood by children in a relative way—at least in the sense that situational and temporal circumstances justify some latitude in the interpretation of values and norms, that expected patterns of behavior can be acted upon in a variety of legitimate ways, and so forth. In this way, mastery at the level of ego (referring to the practical exercise of skill in the attainment of goals) becomes possible, and the gratification of id wishes is at some level legitimated. Superego treats wishes as equivalents to deeds, but with maturation and social contact superego can discriminate degrees of transgression and act accordingly.

To be more specific, the individual internalizes society's mandates on all levels originally in relation to "ideal objects" and "ideal goals." All children possess admired, idealized, omnipotent parents, and all parents hold up to their children cultural ideals (to be cooperative and charitable, or passive, or ambitious, competitive, aggressive, etc.). These ideal objects and goals are transformed by contact with realistic situations, a transformation characterized by a change of aim and object in a process akin to the sublimation of instincts. Thus, an abstraction can take the place of an infantile or childish ideal. Once modified in this way, object love becomes self-love felt as pride and security in the reciprocal fulfillment of standards and expectations, in relation to society and one's own conscience. Ideals are modified by reality (as well as by maturation), and, as ego functions (e.g., judgment, discrimination) mature, distinctions can be made between irrational yearning and realistic necessity. In their modi-

---

[9] Ego ideal may be succinctly defined as "the standard of individual perfection that evokes aspiration." S. Kaplan and R. Whitman, "The Negative Ego-Ideal," *Int. J. Psychoanal.*, 46 (April, 1965): 183. There is a great deal of debate in the psychoanalytic literature as to how or whether superego and ego ideal functions are differentiated, whether ego ideal requires separate theoretical consideration, and so forth. For the present we will assume that superego is differentiated in terms of benevolent and punitive functions, and that the language of ego ideal can be translated as "I ought to behave and be like the person I want to be, so as to be liked by him," while the language of superego can be translated as "I should not behave as I would wish." R. M. Loewenstein, "On the Theory of Superego," in *Psychoanalysis: A General Psychology*, ed. R. M. Loewenstein *et al.* (New York, 1966), p. 303. See also, e.g., Jeanne Lampl-de Groot, "Ego Ideal and Superego," *Psychoanal. Stud. Child*, 17 (1962): 94–106.

fied form these ideals (i.e., "the standards of individual perfection that evoke aspiration") remain the standard by which ego measures its self-worth as well as the satisfaction of both drives and external objects.[10]

This process acquires renewed importance in adolescent resolutions of the identity crisis, one part of which is the decisive detachment from primary (familial) figures and the choice and acceptance of tasks in the wider world. But the problems involved in the process recur continually thereafter as well. In a social-structural sense, and given a level of social stability, the individual passes from one environment to another through time, acquiring new social associations and membership in different groups. At the same time, the individual internalizes new mandates or learns to cope with old ones at new levels of generalization. It is necessary for people to pass through changing degrees of differentiated environments simply as a function of growth; some of this is voluntarily accepted, a lot of it is imposed by the mandates of society. In any event, identity is always in the process of change in the face of socially defined, changing time and space.

But identity changes are imposed also by changing social-structural conditions. In nonrevolutionary situations this means the incorporation of some content previously legitimated for others, which leads to different libidinal positions and different levels of ego and superego development and types of object relationships. Revolutionary changes, as we have noted, alter and redirect identity formation in terms of new patterns and mandates. It is in this situation particularly that the decisive role of the external world must be considered, because such rapid social change occurs outside of awareness (in the sense that events typically develop over time, and with awareness one could perhaps prepare for them) and beyond the possibility for personal control (e.g., in the timing of such events).

The identification and internalization processes are the means by which one learns the values of a society and the ways in which these are expressed, as epitomized in the ways that people work or worship or engage in any social activity that serves to master and control both the external and internal worlds. This is the specifically sociological side of the prob-

---

[10] In the development of superego, limits (which are culturally defined and have meaning in a particular context of standards and expectations) and punishment (which is meted out presumably in the same terms—i.e., realistic punishment) correct the terrifying archaic fantasies of punishment which are conjured by the child in the struggle with his own impulses. This internalized activity enables the child to experience less alienation from real objects, to achieve greater control over impulses, and to achieve modes of expression which are consistent with the mandates of the culture in which he develops.

lem of character—that is, the use made of the goals offered for, and the limitations imposed on, behavior in a context that holds the continuance of organized social life to be a minimum goal. Radical social-structural change is therefore particularly affecting because it threatens not only the transgression of internalized object representations, in the sense that oedipal anxieties are raised again (which may be resolved at the preoedipal level), but also the achieved levels of mastery over all the functions that define everyday individual and group life in society.

We characterize the actual occurrence, the normatively defined experience, of such a situation by the term "object loss"—that is, the loss of an object relationship which disrupts a social context of psychic stability. We briefly defined "object relationship" at an earlier point. Now, however, we want to give this concept, too, a more explicitly sociological definition, relating it concretely to social situations of loss. By object relationship we mean the ties that exist between and among individuals and who- or whatever they invest in their environment with emotional significance. This refers to relationships between and among individuals, between individuals and aspects of their selves (e.g., a sense of efficiency or mastery), and between individuals and such abstract associations and collective arrangements as political authority and organizations, economic institutions, occupational groups, social statuses and roles, and cultural ideals, including standards for the circulation and distribution of resources (e.g., money). Each such object has a history which includes the relationships of other objects associated with it, as well as its prior development in the culture. The importance of this network of relationships is defined by the culture, no matter how else it may be defined idiosyncratically by any individual.[11]

Object loss, then, may be defined as a normatively perceived state of being deprived of, or having to be or do without, some object (person, aspect of self, cultural abstraction) that is invested with affect and is culturally defined as valuable. Loss is a real event, but at the same time

[11] We must emphasize again that, while affect and object relationships in psychoanalytic theory may be centered in the individual, we are now dealing with affect at the social level and as it is culturally defined—that is, as expression obligated by social and cultural standards and as a feature of the give and take that binds group members. It is only when affect is shared and exchanged in this manner that matters can be conceived of as being justly or unjustly dealt with, or that standards can be interpreted as having been violated. Thus, no matter how important affect is in individual terms (with regard to self-cathexis, as a signal function, etc.), it is those aspects of self that are socially shared which are affected by failure at the social level. Moreover, we have already noted that internalization processes affect every level of personality. This means, too, that personal activities are defined in terms of social consequences, and so at best only a few personal actions do not have meaning for social stability and change.

it is a perception in terms of which the individual endows the event with symbolic significance. Even the passing of some familiar form of oppression can be felt as a loss if such a form provided one with a sense of mastery and if there had been some secondary gain derived from it (e.g., as with certain nurturant and protective obligations of authority in traditional structures).[12]

For the individual, the experience of loss, including all situations of being hurt, disappointed, or neglected, is responded to idiosyncratically in a variety of ways (e.g., sorrow, grief, depression, anxiety, guilt, shame, helplessness, hopelessness, denial, relief, or by the absence of feeling). For the individual, too, the most profound personal experience of loss is that of a loved or valued person. However, in the maturational sense, everyone has experienced loss, whether in the separation of self from mother or in the later resolutions of oedipal, adolescent, and identity crises, and so forth.[13] Societies provide institutionalized means of coping with these typical experiences. Still, they have an enormous impact: loss

---

[12] On object loss, see David Peretz, "Development, Object-Relationship, and Loss," in *Loss and Grief: Psychological Management in Medical Practise*, ed. Bernard Schoenberg *et al.* (New York, 1970), pp. 3–19; and Gregory Rochlin, *Griefs and Discontents* (Boston, 1965), *passim;* see also, e.g., I. Yahalom, "Sense, Affect, and Image in Development of the Symbolic Process," *Int. J. Psychoanal.*, 48 (1967). On the views of English psychoanalysts, who place special emphasis on the problem of loss, see Myer Mendelson, *Psychoanalytic Concepts of Depression* (Springfield, Ill., 1960), p. 91. For a variety of relevant statements on the recent upsurge in the literature on this problem, on Freud's experience with it, and so on, see the following: Margaret Mahler, "Notes on the Development of Basic Moods," in *Psychoanalysis*, ed. Loewenstein *et al.*, p. 156; George R. Krupp, "Identification as a Defense against Anxiety in Coping with Loss," *Int. J. Psychoanal.*, 46 (July, 1965): 304; and *idem*, "The Bereavement Reaction: A Special Case of Separation Anxiety," in *The Psychoanalytic Study of Society*, ed. W. Muensterberger and S. Axelrad, 4 vols. (New York, 1960–67), 2: 42; John Bowlby, "Processes of Mourning," *Int. J. Psychoanal.*, 42 (July–October, 1961): 323; George H. Pollock, "Mourning and Adaptation," *ibid.*, pp. 343–44.

"Object relationship," and "object loss" are not the happiest phrases; but they are useful insofar as "object" refers not only to people. Causes and organizations, not to mention position and possessions, are just as likely to be invested with intense emotional commitment.

[13] On the experience of loss in separation, see Margaret Mahler, "Thoughts about Development and Individuation," *Psychoanal. Stud. Child*, 18 (1963): 309, among others; Fred Pine and Manuel Furer, "Studies of the Separation-Individuation Phase," *ibid.*, pp. 325–26; Margaret Mahler and Manuel Furer, "Certain Aspects of the Separation-Individuation Phase," *Psychoanal. Quart.*, 32 (1963): 1–14; Margaret Mahler and Kitty La Perriere, "Mother-Child during Separation-Individuation," *ibid.*, 34 (1965): 483–98. On the resolution of oedipal conflict as a prototype of loss and of the mourning process, see Hans W. Loewald, "Internalization, Separation, Mourning, and the Superego," *ibid.*, 31 (1962): 483–504. On adolescence, e.g., see Martha Wolfenstein, "How is Mourning Possible," *Psychoanal. Stud. Child*, 21 (1966): 93–126; Joan Fleming and Sol Altschul, "Activation of Mourning and Growth by Psychoanalysis," *Int. J. Psychoanal.*, 44 (October, 1963): 429.

in maturational terms seems to have a variety of residual effects, one being a held-over fear of situations of potential traumatic content.[14] All these different experiences of loss are not carried forward simply as the recollection of events; rather, they become focal points of conflict which, set into motion, affect the formation of character, give rise to a variety of defensive and adaptive reactions, and otherwise govern behavior to a significant extent.[15] Thus, both the events and the behaviors mobilized to bring them under control (make them ego-syntonic) persist and endure consciously and unconsciously, affecting subsequent behavior for both good and ill.

It is important for us to note—and Freud pointed this out in *Mourning and Melancholia*[16]—that the loss of an abstract object relationship (e.g., traditional rights or authority structures, a cultural ideal, a role or status, etc.) has a similar impact on individual experience. Such loss will undoubtedly constitute changes in relationships symbolic of past (actual or threatened) loss. The more important point, however, is that when such loss occurs as a result of social-structural changes, groups of people will be systematically affected, and it is on this basis that a sociological definition of object loss is possible. For our purposes, object loss can be sociologically defined as the inability of groups of people to translate internalized mandates into behavior as traditional and culturally sanctioned forms of behavior become—for whatever structural reason—unavailable, ineffective, or dysfunctional as a result of social change.

What must be stressed in these terms is that *any* network of object relationships (keeping in mind our emphasis on the cultural meanings of objects, internalized symbolic meanings—in brief, standards and expec-

---

[14] Peter Blos, "Character Formation in Adolescence," *Psychoanal. Stud. Child*, 23 (1968): 254. "Such sensitization to special danger situations of a permanent traumatic valence are to be found, for example, in object loss, passive dependency, loss of control, decline of self-esteem." Actual and threatened experiences of loss, and the various kinds of response to these experiences, as these occur developmentally, are assimilated and integrated in personality. That is, adaptive and defensive techniques are elaborated which enable the individual both to deal with loss as a possible opportunity for enhanced personal autonomy and to cope with any subsequent experience without being overwhelmed by it. However, a special sensitivity to the possibility of loss always remains: object loss represents a danger situation which has a permanent traumatic capacity. Separation anxiety, depression, as well as fears of passive dependency, loss of control, and damaged self-esteem, are dynamically linked in these terms.

[15] "Whereas the oedipus conflicts evoke libidinal repression, the loss complex and oedipal conflicts together bring about the elaboration of ego's defenses." Rochlin, *Griefs and Discontents*, pp. 191, 236. See also Blos, "Character Formation in Adolescence," p. 292; Kurt R. Eissler, "Notes upon the Emotionality of a Schizophrenic Patient . . . ," *Psychoanal. Stud. Child*, 7 (1954): 204. Past experience, of course, can strengthen or compromise the ability to cope.

[16] In "Mourning and Melancholia" (14: 243) Freud raised a serious problem with regard to change in these terms. But in this work he was far more intent on understanding superego than on understanding the problem of social change.

tations rather than real object ties) constitutes a social context of psychic support and gives meaning to everyday situations. The loss of an object relationship (i.e., the inability to act on internalized evaluative or moral standards, on ego standards for achievement and for drive gratification) means the loss of a system of support—that is, the loss of everyday contexts for action and meaning, the loss of a sense of membership, the inability of individuals to assert and affirm identity—and therefore a situation of psychic and social instability. Such a situation can arise for any group of people in relation to any institutional structure; historically, different groups of people at different times have made demands against the religious, political, economic, familial, and educational establishments.[17]

Moreover, this process must be understood in the terms employed by Durkheim in his explanation of *anomie*. That is, the normative perception of loss may result from the decline or narrowing of expected courses of action, or it may result from an increase in expected courses of action. Because moves in either direction must affect the ability to act on internalized patterns of behavior, both possibilities are disruptive of stability. The classic question of whether revolutions occur when things are getting better or when they are getting worse must be answered in the light of this assertion. Both possibilities must be considered, *and which of the two was the effective cause can be determined only by an analysis of each instance.*

In addition, it should be understood that responses to situations of loss in either case can run the gamut from apathy, withdrawal, resignation, and despair to active demands for the restoration or retention of traditional mandates, through active demands for a greater degree of autonomy and inclusion in decision-making processes, to an exhilarating sense of liberation and omnipotent fantasies of unlimited accomplishment.[18] Loss may be experienced as deprivation or as the signal for a greater degree

---

[17] See, e.g., Charles A. Pinderhughes, "Somatic, Psychic, and Social Sequelae of Loss," *J. Amer. Psychoanal. Ass.*, 19, no. 4 (October, 1971): 690; Jules V. Coleman, "Adaptive Integration of Psychiatric Symptoms in Ego Regulation," *Archives of General Psychiatry*, 24 (1971): 20. It should be noted that such experiences of loss are situationally and institutionally specific and realistic and justifiable in the light of structural failures, disruptions, or dysfunctions. The responses to loss, however, will vary—as noted above.

[18] The alternative of apathy, resignation, and despair is a common one for individuals, but it occurs at the group level too, and so it must be accounted for. Situations of loss which affect all institutional levels at once, in which contexts of support in all areas are massively disrupted, will produce this result. When ego perceives that a feared traumatic event has occurred, that nothing it can do can alter or affect an outcome, a sense of helplessness and hopelessness will follow. This is what happened to many Jews in the concentration camp experience. All contexts of support were disrupted, it was clear that no help was forthcoming from any quarter, and there was no way to interrupt the events; no adequate defense was possible. We may understand this in terms of narcissistic shock, destroyed self-esteem, and the complete violation of identity.

of freedom, the demands for which can occur in either a moderate or a radical form.[19]

We cannot go at length into the question of why people react one way or another to situations of loss. This is a very complex problem which involves the vicissitude of affects we usually associate with object loss, affects which shape attachments to leaders and ideology, to cognitive capacities and orientations, time orientations (i.e., to past and future), to aggression, hierarchy, and so on. Every society has culturally constituted defense mechanisms that help people deal with the loss of loved individuals. But no society can instruct its citizens in the potential loss of cherished patterns of social behavior—that is, in the possibility that the values and norms of society itself may be rendered ineffectual or dysfunctional, thereby necessitating basic social change. This would require that a society hold its values to be relative, and this would, at the least, render the socialization process chaotic. It is true that there may be a great deal of flexibility in the interpretation of codes, and aspects of the morality may come under conscious control. But, ultimately, values have to be expressed in absolute terms and are apprehended more fundamentally in moral terms than in cognitive terms. In this lies a fundamental contradiction: what must be conceived of as sacred and timeless is actually relative to changing social processes and requirements. Thus, even if questions of interest did not intervene (and definitions of interest are themselves affectually based), radical change would still precipitate conflict. It is

---

[19] Loewald, "Internalization, Separation, Mourning, and the Superego," p. 490. Passive resignation or demands to restore a traditional morality occur when object loss leads to a sense of helplessness or to a dread of the violated object, and so on. For object loss to be taken as the opportunity for increased autonomy, some such content had already to have been internalized, or some valued person had to have been held up as an ideal—perhaps an economic or religious content or figure. But there must be something extant at some level which can be recovered, refined, and cathected. I. P. Glauber, "Federn's Annotation of Freud's Theory of Anxiety," *J. Amer. Psychoanal. Ass.*, 11, no. 1 (January, 1963): 88; Elizabeth R. Zetzel, "Depression and the Incapacity to Bear It," in *Drives, Affects, Behavior*, vol. 2, ed. Max Schur (New York, 1953), p. 258.
    It is in these terms too that our statements in Chapter I on Marx and alienation should be understood. In Marx's view the increasing development of capitalism narrowed the workers' courses of action and led to increasing isolation from objects and systems of support (i.e., to object loss). Following Freud's concept of phase-appropriate anxiety, we pushed Marx's thoughts on loss to their logical conclusion. The increasing sense of alienation, the ever-ramifying experience of loss, uninterrupted and progressive, could never lead to class-conscious action. It has led to apathy, withdrawal, and depression. Thus, men act to the degree that they are integrated and not alienated. This experience of integration may be at a very low level (predicated on denial and projection, e.g.); it may mean following a man like Hitler. Still, no matter how regressed such action is, it is based on integration and not alienation. See G. M. Platt and F. Weinstein, "Alienation and the Problem of Social Action," in *The Phenomenon of Sociology*, ed. Edward Tiryakian (New York, 1971).

because there apparently cannot be any widespread conscious control over this information, and because no social patterns are ever worked out to facilitate the transition from one mode of social organization to another, that revolution has emerged so centrally as a form of social change. Moreover, this means too that each situation must be treated anew and is experienced as traumatic each time. Hence, violence, moral outrage, the tug of war between past and future, acceptance or denial of loss, and different types of leadership and ideology arise as expressions of these various possibilities.[20]

We can, however, point out some dimensions of the problem and in general terms indicate some behavioral differences involved in treating loss as deprivation or in accepting it as an opportunity for enhanced autonomy. With regard to the former alternative, there are situations in which the context of a stable sense of self is excessively disrupted—that is, to a greater degree than the ego can cope with in realistic terms. To the extent that a threat has materialized and appears to be overwhelming in its consequences, stability can be achieved again only through the reattachment of ideals to real, external, but idealized objects, the reunion in archaic terms with an object via ideology and action.[21] The ego, in other words, must attempt to pursue an integrating course, even if this means dependent submission to external authority. The criteria of ego ideal tension, for example (i.e., narcissism, projection of aggression, illogical thinking), are forms of behavior perpetuated by normatively perceived object loss, and they serve as restitutional measures on which continued ego integration depends. Men struggle in difficult situations to retain a sense of control and purpose, and, if men are forced to surrender to an intolerable aspect of reality, they must, or they will, try to use even that surrender as a basis for integration and renewed activity. When abstract ideals cannot be maintained, primitive ideals must serve.

[20] George H. Pollock, "On Mourning and Anniversaries: The Relationship of Culturally Constituted Defensive Systems to Intrapsychic Adaptive Processes," *The Israel Annals of Psychiatry and Related Disciplines*, 10, no. 1 (March, 1972): 9–40.

[21] If such a threat is so overwhelming that it must be passively accepted as inevitable, depression will result. However, rather than tolerate such withdrawal, people will struggle and use whatever means of support available. A sociological position on this alternative can be organized on the basis of the following literature: Edward Bibring, "The Mechanism of Depression," in *Affective Disorders*, ed. Phyllis Greenacre (New York, 1953), pp. 34–35; Zetzel, "Depression and the Incapacity to Bear It," pp. 247–48; and Mahler, "Notes on the Development of Basic Moods," p. 156. See also Blos, "Character Formation in Adolescence," p. 254; Arthur H. Schmale, Jr., "A Genetic View of Affects," *Psychoanal. Stud. Child*, 19 (1964): 287–88; G. Piers and M. Singer, *Shame and Guilt* (Springfield, Ill., 1953), pp. 11, 16; Jacob A. Arlow, "Unconscious Fantasy and Disturbances of Conscious Experience," *Psychoanal. Quart.*, 38, no. 1 (1969): 1, 16.

It follows, of course, that at this level the possibility of choosing which objects one will be dependent on or independent of is lost. Commitment to external authority in the terms described is not only reassuring, it is necessary, and self-sacrifice and the jeopardy of interest are preferred to any further possible experience of abandonment or failure. This is, in ideal typical terms, one way in which men "escape from freedom." Persistent threats from the external world, particularly when it becomes clear that the ego by its own efforts cannot master these threats, will force the regression of drives to pregenital stages and the regression of ego and superego functions as well.[22] Submission to a leader (or to authority generally) abates anxiety both in terms of the social world and in terms of the dominance of pregenital wishes (from whence comes the capacity for violence); but such submission also precludes any independent activity or objective analysis of the environment.

Two further consequences of this situation also can be readily identified. First, there is a manifest absence of ambivalence with regard to ideology and authority. If ambivalence cannot be expressed, one object is cathected with reverence and all aggression is directed to someone or something outside. That is, authority cannot be apprehended as both good and bad at the same time. This need to idealize authority establishes the possibility for a "pregenital" milieu, a world of narcissistic entitlement, in which the "bad" can be treated as brutally as anxiety and devotion to the "good" require, and in which the difference between life and death is obscured and the removal of "sources of tension" does not have the emotional significance ordinarily associated with death. This kind of behavior is compatible with running a highly technical, mechanized industrial establishment; there is no inherent contradiction between regressive commitments to authority and the continued manipulation of skills. This is

---

[22] "If disintegration or regression occur lower levels of organization take over control at lower levels of integration, with behavior and thought more characteristic of primary process function." The response at this level, as we observed earlier, is not to fear of the wrath of superego or of mutilation, but to fear of abandonment and ego dissolution. Seymour L. Lustman, "Impulse Control, Structure, and the Synthetic Function," in *Psychoanalysis*, ed. Loewenstein *et al.*, p. 205. Anna Freud distinguishes between temporal regression, which occurs in relation to aim-directed impulses, object representations, and fantasy content, and topographical and formal regression, which involves ego functions, secondary thought processes, reality principle, and so on. A topographical regression produces hallucinatory wish fulfillments in the place of rational thinking; a temporal regression harks back to older psychic structures; a formal regression causes primitive methods of expression and representation to take the place of contemporary ones. Regression in these terms occurs and can be identified at the levels of thought, feeling, defense, and in relation to external object ties. Anna Freud, *Normality and Pathology in Childhood* (New York, 1965), p. 95.

especially the case as the revered leader provides the cues which will be responded to.[23]

Second, aggression and rigidity assume a global form in this way because the figures, objects, and standards adhered to or attacked are no longer simply perceived as being tied to the political and economic world. Rather, activity is fused and confused with past traumatic experiences, with threats of loss, forbidden wishes, and so on, and the whole world is implicated because at this level the familial past has been evoked. The response is total because the wider social structures (and the people involved in them) are treated with the rage, the idealization, and the lack of separation and discrimination which was evident in early childhood. In brief, "Aggression directed against the whole world concerns primarily . . . the first environment, in which the 'whole world' was represented then, by the siblings and father as well as the mother."[24]

Loss, then, may be responded to in thought and action aimed at the recovery or restoration of some past (but idealized and hence distorted) state, and may be characterized by a litigious search for compensation. But loss can also be the occasion for testing internal and external reality, and on this basis illusions about, and affective ties to, authority or to any association or structure can be relinquished.[25] The ego measures its capacities against the situation and may feel equipped to meet and master the experience. Efforts in this direction—codified in demands for freedom and self-assertion—certainly cannot all be interpreted as defensive.

These different reactions to loss may be understood as strategies in the service of identity. A significant discrepancy between what one actually is, or must become or do, and the ideal representation of self, if it is not corrected, leads to feelings of self-hatred, unworthiness, and the like. It must be emphasized, therefore, that, if a group of people hitherto excluded from participation in decision-making processes develops—for whatever reasons—areas of competence and novel forms of expertise, and

[23] Edith Jacobson, *The Self and the Object World* (New York, 1964), p. 44; Margaret Mahler and Manuel S. Furer, *On Human Symbiosis and the Vicissitudes of Individuation*, 2 vols. (New York, 1968), 1: 60–61.

[24] Sandor Lorand, "Therapy of Depressive States," in *The Meaning of Despair*, ed. W. Gaylin (New York, 1968), p. 324. This is an older essay, and at present the mother would come first, not last, almost as an afterthought. See also Peter Neubauer, "Trauma and Psychopathology," in *Psychic Trauma*, ed. Sidney Furst (New York, 1968), pp. 94–95). The omnipotent demands against the environment cannot, of course, be met, and so there is resistance. But this results from incorrect estimates of the true situation by an impaired ego.

[25] Paul G. Meyerson, "Assimilation of Unconscious Material," *Int. J. Psychoanal.*, 44 (July, 1963): 320; Loewald, "Internalization, Separation, Mourning, and the Superego," p. 490.

if the sources and symbols of prestige do not then become systematically available, and the social structure does not change to account for changed emotional relationships, including changed perceptions of self, it may become too anxiety provoking for people *not* to revolt.[26] In response to such a situation new or more generalized mandates and more inclusive social structures are organized.

A variety of factors are involved in the capacity to achieve a greater degree of freedom on the basis of such a revolt. This implies first that individuals can cathect their own cognitive and moral capacities, as well as their affectual experience.[27] If self-willed cognitive and moral capacities are compromised by the fear of affect, the organization of another type of rigid and violent social order will follow.[28] When the ability to retain control over the environment depends upon the repression (or isolation) of feeling, the value of thought processes is exaggerated.[29] On the one hand, this results typically in a forceful emphasis on the manipulation of the external world, fostering logical analysis and observation in a restricted way (i.e., cognitive capacities are substituted for emotional signals). But, on the other hand, this results in the application of more rational and manipulative criteria to people and to ego-oriented rationalizations for this behavior. From this follows the impression that the whole world can be made to submit to technique. Ego capacities are highly regarded, but the attempt to build a world to match that high regard ends in another kind of distortion.

The achievement of a greater degree of freedom also implies the ability of individuals and groups to bring the past under control. The "failures" of the past, and especially the behavioral styles, must be assimilated,

---

[26] "One of the most important functions of the ego is to come to terms with the culture in which the individual finds himself and to make some sort of adaptation to it, even if the adaptation takes the form of rebellion." W. H. Gillespie, "Neurotic Ego Distortions," *Int. J. Psychoanal.*, 39 (1958): 258. It is, of course, a myth that psychoanalysis is organized to integrate individuals into a given social order no matter what. From a psychoanalytic point of view there are obviously very dysfunctional forms of conformity and compliance, and very syntonic forms of rebellion.

[27] See Leo A. Spiegel, "Affect in Relation to Self and Object," *Psychoanal. Stud. Child*, 21 (1966): 85.

[28] According to one definition, "Autonomy means psychological separation from the maternal object, and the associated socialization of aggression." Charles N. Sarlin, "Identity, Culture, and Psychosexual Development," *American Imago*, 24 no. 3 (Fall, 1967): 197. See also the introduction to F. Weinstein and G. M. Platt, *The Wish To Be Free* (Berkeley and Los Angeles, 1970), for a definition of "maternal" in these terms. The problem has also been discussed in terms of "active and passive." See Michael Walzer, *The Revolution of the Saints* (Cambridge, Mass., 1965), pp. 1–21.

[29] See S. C. Miller, "Ego Autonomy in Sensory Deprivation, Isolation and Stress," *Int. J. Psychoanal.*, 43 (January–February, 1962): 13.

integrated, and rationalized without excessive anxiety because in a codified form this past serves as the determination of limitations and restrictions on self and others in the new social order. What one must not be or do is defined partly in terms of the past. However, this implies also an ability to tolerate or accept a degree of powerlessness in the present, as this inevitably exists for all people as they interact with one another. At the cognitive level this means a plural definition of self and class interest and a tolerance for ambiguous situations.

This view of the interplay between social- and psychic-structural events is better articulated to empirical realities from a number of standpoints. In the terms we have outlined it is possible to account not only for the activities of obvious interest groups but for the activities of any group that is distinguished by a role or status and that is differentiated along some line (age, sex, race, occupation, etc.). It is also possible to explain the occurrence of change within a value structure, as well as change in opposition to that structure; to account for all the behavioral manifestations that may occur in either case; and to account for the organization of movements that have sought change on all institutional levels at one time or another. It is also possible to explain why all such movements give rise to moderate, radical, and reactionary wings—whether the groups involved have a primary, or only a derived, relationship to economic structures, or whether they are aimed explicitly at the political level or at power relationships on some other institutional level. A descriptive and analytic scheme based on the structurally imposed conflicts of two classes—particularly in that these classes are defined by their relationship to the modes of production, and their action is understood to be determined by that relationship—is certainly inadequate. The critical determinants of behavior are not primarily class or interest; rather, the processes of internalization and object loss give rise to the widest possible range of affectual, cognitive, and evaluative behavior. Given this framework, it follows that neither role (e.g., leaders and followers) nor class (e.g., workers and owners) can be considered as the fundamental problem.

In these different ways, then, social- and psychic-structural events are interwoven, and any analysis that does not encompass both elements must be inadequate and incomplete. With regard to proceeding in historical and social analysis, a number of specific points follow from the basic frame of reference and these should be made explicit. The most important of these, particularly with regard to problems of change, is the necessity to investigate first the effects of social-structural events—industrialization, urbanization, bureaucratization, and the like—on the ability of groups of people to act in terms of internalized patterns of behavior. The differences between ongoing, stable social situations and situations of systematic radical change revolve on this point.

It follows from this that social change can never stem from the idiosyncratic wishes and activities of unique leaders. Great men may emerge in crisis situations, but they do not cause them, and they are effective in them only to the extent that they can interpret adequately to those involved the specific crisis, its causes and solutions. This interpretation may be essentially realistic or wishfully distorted, or both at the same time. But the primary function of such leaders is to express in a summary way the actual experience of masses of people and to abate the anxiety caused by the experience of loss. Thus a leader may serve to maintain among people a coherent sense of self and a coherent identity in a time of stress; or he may encourage the internalization of new mandates and the formation of a changed identity in a transitional period; or he may even be necessary to prevent ego dissolution and breakdown in a time of extraordinary crisis. But he does not originate the situation in which these things occur, and his behavior must be interpreted in the light of the larger events.

As we wrote earlier, psychohistorians tend to concentrate on the study of elite figures, and this stems in part from an implicit but mistaken assumption that the behavior of the mass can be inferred from the behavior of the leader. It is assumed that the common man follows a leader and acts on a developing doctrine (religious, political, economic, or even artistic and scientific) because the leader possesses "gifts of grace." In the leader and his doctrine the follower presumably sees his own ideal self. But this is not enough, on theoretical and empirical grounds, to explain the connection between the two. It is more accurate to assume that the rank and file follow for a variety of reasons, which can be expressed in structural terms (id, ego, and superego), and that different groups within a mass have different notions of what is important. If we say that the leader expresses for the common man what he has already experienced and needs to bring under control, this should be understood in a broad sense to encompass a wide range of experiences and interests. Moreover, we must understand the problem of the leader largely in the sense that Freud understood the problem of the artist and sublimation. All people sublimate, but what forces shape the peculiar genius of the artist Freud could not say. The point is that the historian is more likely to be able to determine the social conditions from which one or another leader has emerged, as well as the reasons why such a man was able to attract a following, than he is to determine what finally made a man a leader.

It follows from this too that such situations as we describe are not in the first place the result of intellectual apprehension or influence. These problems of order and change, or the relationship of the individual to society in these terms, cannot be comprehended in primarily intellectual terms. Searching out how one writer or activist was influenced by earlier examples is merely a refined intellectual game, and is really quite irrelevant for analysis, unless and until the social factors are identified which make some idiosyncratic insight of the past relevant to some subsequent event involving concerted social action. It is necessary to understand how social events mobilize psychic responses in such a way that one particular idea resonates emotionally rather than another. Robespierre was affected by Rousseau, Lenin by Marx or Chernyshevski, and Hitler by Wagner and Houston Stewart Chamberlain not only in intellectual terms, as a function of conscious, deliberate, reasoned, cognitive appraisal. Whether and to what extent action was facilitated or hampered by id, ego, or superego motives, or to what extent guilt and anxiety led to the distortion of reality, or the absence of these affective responses led to rather objective analysis of the environment (or, as explained above, to another type of distortion) can be understood only in terms of developing normative reactions to external events.[30] Only after the social events are connected to psychic responses is it practicable to identify some individual in the past as having served as a model, or as having exercised "influence."

To be more specific, it does not matter how many books, tracts, and pamphlets have been written exhorting people to one or another type of action; until the social conditions for change are extant, no *movement* can result. That is, *until the emotional bases for compliance have been threatened or eroded by social events*, no systematic, codified social action can follow. Thus the primary and indispensable task of the investigator is to examine the effects of social events on obligated expressions of emotion and on internalized standards and expectations. The answer to the question of why social structures remain (relatively) stable—even when subordination and exploitation are evident—lies in the identification of the kinds of emotional

[30] Radical activists are a special kind of people in some ways; yet in other ways they go about the business of revolution not much differently from the way an average man goes about his daily tasks. Human actors, radical or not, are in no position to assess rationally the historical past or their present environment as if they were performing scientific experiments, then justifying and giving a logical direction to action on the basis of their "findings." As we have already noted, many, perhaps most, bases of action are not available for conscious examination, and conscious expressions about the ultimate worthiness of a given social order are much more typically moral than they are cognitive. Men achieve insight into social processes and they are capable of organizing personal and social activity in terms of this insight. But in the final analysis this insight is expressed and passed on, for the most part, as something "sacred" and as something that is not open for general discussion, much less for repudiation.

gratification that inhibit critical insight into one's social position (and thereby make dependence tolerable). The answer to the question of when subordination, for example, comes to be viewed as illegitimate and intolerable lies in the identification of changing social conditions that interrupt or terminate particular patterns of emotional gratification.

In these psychosocial terms there follows the necessity of understanding both the nature of reality orientations (which requires relating the psychoanalytic ego psychology to sociological formulations of symbolic control, values, norms, patterns of appropriate action, and so on) and the implications that wishful and distorted behavior have for action. Both realistic and regressive types of behavior must be accounted for and, in spite of certain tendencies in psychoanalysis, the former cannot be reduced to the latter. It can also be argued psychoanalytically that realistic and regressive motives are involved in every action. But it is necessary to distinguish between the two, and it is possible to define which was paramount.[31]

However, this is a more difficult and complex task than is usually conceded, involving as it does the interpretation of an interpretive process. It is necessary to describe in historical terms what in fact happened at a particular point, but it is also necessary to describe how (if not why) something happened. This means understanding the emotional commitments of other, often remote, individuals and groups. The psychosocial method is indispensable for this type of analysis, but at least four basic errors typically occur and therefore tend to distort interpretations.

One error is the analysis of past events in the light of contemporary bases of action—that is, the definition of behavior which may be deemed inappropriate at this point to have always been inappropriate (i.e., "neurotic," "regressive"). More specifically, the problem is one of failing to define the primacies for the bases of action, primacies which are rooted in somatic and psychic processes, but also in social structure, and which therefore are subject to change. Cognitive orientations, for example, have up to now been decisive for integration in modern societies. The systematic development and cathexis of cognitive processes leads to a particular type of mastery over self and environment. But this is not the only way to apprehend and master reality, and cognitive orientations have not always been the most appropriate or adaptive posture in other times and places. Moreover, if the emphasis on cognitive processes inhibits a variety of

---

[31] As we pointed out earlier, every action can be said to be gratifying in terms of id, ego, and superego. See, e. g., H. Hartmann, E. Kris, and R. M. Loewenstein, "Culture and Personality," *Papers*, p. 113; Schafer, "Ideals, Ego Ideal, and Ideal Self," p. 141.

possible emotional ties, particular types of distortion will follow, and these too will not have been the same in other times and places.[32]

A second error is the definition of behavior in libidinal or drive terms exclusively or primarily—that is, the failure to pursue analysis along the parallel tracks of drive organization, affectual response, ego and superego development, and object relationships. The earlier emphasis in psycho-analysis on drives, early maturational stages, the vicissitudes of oedipal conflict, and symptom formation led many interested writers to attempt solutions to problems that were not consistent with historical and socio-logical endeavor. Freud himself had repeatedly though randomly sug-gested that there were other dimensions to the problem, particularly at the social level. But these suggestions were not picked up and perhaps could not have been until various aspects of theory had been amplified in the context of the ego psychology. Thus, as early as 1907, for example, Freud identified certain analogous forms of behavior in obsessive indi-viduals and in the character of religious practices. "The most essential similarity would reside in the underlying renunciation of the activation of instincts that are constitutionally present; the chief differences would be in the nature of those instincts which in the neurosis are exclusively sexual in their origins *while in the religion, they spring from egoistic sources.*"

Freud here was making a distinction in terms of an older duality: sexual instincts and ego instincts (which for convenience' sake we may equate with self-preservative instincts). Perhaps Freud would not later have argued that religious practices derive from essentially nonsexual sources. But he had already raised the question of the fate of sexual aims and objects at the group level and had introduced the concept of identi-fication to deal with the dilemma. Moreover, if we translate "ego instincts" into the language of ego psychology—that is, adaptive and defensive

[32] As a general mode of behavior, of course, cognitive orientations have always been available. We are talking about *primacies*, however, and not generalities. One way of looking at the problem is this: It is possible for individuals in this society to be con-sidered successful and to be granted respect and admiration in political, economic, religious, military, educational, or familial spheres of activity on the basis of a punitive and perfectionist superego and on the basis of the repression of unconscious conflicts, which are controlled by inhibitory or phobic behaviors. Such individuals will boast of their self-control, "objectivity," their ability to suffer hardships, and so forth. The society so values these qualities that their exaggeration (and the repression of feeling) may easily be regarded as a positive virtue. And, in fact, such people are peculiarly capable of fulfilling a variety of important tasks in this society because the cognitive orientation to action is primary. This would not be the case in other times and places. We might also point out that contemporary commitments to erotic, expressive, aes-thetic, and religious modes could challenge and modify the primacy of ego functions in this society.

techniques, reality testing, secondary autonomy, and the like (which are structured by identification)—it is clear that there is a social component in the type of behavior Freud dealt with. The persistent emphasis on drive resulted from Freud's interests and from the problems he had to solve as his discoveries unfolded. It is a mistake to continue that emphasis in historical and sociological work in the light of what is now known.

This is underscored by the realization that the effects of social structure on personality have primarily to do with control, vulnerability to disruption, a sense of future intactness, continuity, self-sameness, and factors of this order. What we see in the analysis above (dealing with loss in deprivation) are reactions to threatened integrity, reflections of a grandiose self, reactions to helplessness, expressions of rage, ways of recovering narcissistic balance, and regression, not only in terms of drive, but also in terms of ego and superego and object relationships. Although it is possible to identify drive components in this type of behavior, this is not the same as saying that the fundamental problem is frustration over drive tensions, or that our attention must be focused primarily on drive manifestations.[33]

This error can be avoided by establishing for oneself a series of criteria related to specific times and places and organized in such terms as the definition of the types of ego ideals and superego mandates presented (i.e., what it is that one should strive to be; in what ways one should not behave as one would wish), and a definition of whether ego functions (such as cognitive orientations) are consistent with these. It is also necessary to define what it means to feel good, admirable, worthy, and secure in a given society, not only in terms of living up to the morality, but also in terms of work and the mastery of skills; in light of these factors it then becomes possible to determine how self-esteem and narcissistic integrity are

---

[33] Freud, "Obsessive Acts and Religious Practises," 9: 126–27; italics added. It should be pointed out that Freud did deal with religion subsequently—for example, in *The Future of an Illusion*—in terms of man's helplessness and the necessity of defending himself against the crushingly superior forces of nature. This, as we observed earlier, also brings up identification and object relational processes and is not an argument based exclusively on drive manifestations. See the discussion in Henri Parens and Leon J. Saul, *Dependence in Man* (New York, 1971), pp. 23–28. See also David A. Freedman, "The Genesis of Obsessional Phenomena," *Psychoanal. Rev.*, 58, no. 3 (1971): 367; Adrienne Applegarth, "Comments on Aspects of the Theory of Psychic Energy," *J. Amer. Psychoanal. Ass.*, 19, no. 3 (July, 1971): 383; Burton N. Wixen, "Grudges: A Psychoanalytic Study," *Psychoanal. Rev.*, 58, no. 3 (1971): 343; Arnold Goldberg, "On Waiting," *Int. J. Psychoanal.*, 52 (1971): 413–21; Louis Miller, "Identity and Violence," *The Israel Annals of Psychiatry and Related Disciplines*, 10, no. 1 (March, 1972): 75. Many scholars, of course, denied the usefulness of psychoanalysis generally, or for the study of groups, the historical past, and so forth. No doubt resistance accounts for some, and maybe even a lot, of this. But there were and are plenty of real and substantial reasons for taking this position.

maintained or how these processes are likely to be disrupted and with what possible results. Furthermore, it is necessary to specify the types of relationships to authority that are encouraged (i.e., the extent to which people are dependent on, or independent of, different authorities in their environment, which is identified in the extent to which public and private morality are congruent, in the kind of analysis of authority that is possible, and especially in whether both the good and bad features of authority can be assimilated and therefore accepted or challenged).[34] These criteria, of course, are meant to be illustrative of an approach to historical and sociological issues, not an exhaustive list of problem areas.

A third error, and one which rather easily merges with ideological bias and with certain strong tendencies in the psychoanalytic literature, results from viewing behavior, especially behavior involved in responses to social change, as regressive in the strictly pejorative sense of that term. For example, psychoanalysts conventionally speak of the transgression of morality, the violation of internalized mandates, in the language of guilt —that is, in terms of an internalized threat which attaches to wrongdoing. This affectual process in response to violation is based initially on the origin of the superego function within the family and in reference to the superior power of the parents. In this situation the primary motive force for identification with the values and attitudes of the parents is the fear of castration. But there is more than one type of identification, and, insofar as identification may also derive from "any new perception of a common quality shared with some other person," this process can influence behavior at any point in life, as we have observed.

This latter type of identification, which involves the emulation of admired persons, particularly in a sociological sense, since this includes "educators, teachers, people chosen as ideal models," refers to the incorporation and development of ego ideal. The threat attached to failure with regard to ego ideal, as well as the types of affective response, are different from the threat and response to superego transgression. However, in the psychoanalytic literature the problem of superego is discussed much more extensively than the problem of ego ideal (just as guilt is discussed much more often than shame). Thus, while it is obviously necessary to take both

[34] See, e.g., Bibring, "The Mechanism of Depression," pp. 24–25, 37–39. When the psychoanalytic statements here are recast in sociological terms, our meaning of "primacies" and the forms these might assume, as well as a variety of possible orientations to authority and the reasons for the emphasis on self-esteem, identity, ideals, and prohibitions, will become clearer. The material is too extensive to quote handily here. Moreover, it should be said that we mention psychoanalytic contributions such as this one because they are suggestive, not because they are definitive. In these terms see also, e.g., Otto Kernberg, "A Psychoanalytic Classification of Character Pathology," *J. Amer. Psychoanal. Ass.*, 18, no. 4 (October, 1970): 800–822.

aspects of the problem into account, one's attention is constantly focused on superego and guilt.[35]

The most important result of the failure to distinguish between, and to deal with, both manifestations is that the self-punitive functions of super-ego have been overemphasized, while the self-protective functions of superego have been neglected. Because of this merging of interest and bias, radical action aimed at adjusting to changed social circumstances has typically been interpreted along the lines of oedipal aggression, as if no reality factors are, or even can be, involved. But it is necessary to consider how people will protect themselves in different situations, or the different ways in which they may declare their readiness to accept a greater degree of personal responsibility in adapting to new conditions. Radical change in psychoanalytic terms cannot have only the negative, punitive implication.

Thus, while it is true that the threatened ego falls back onto more primitive modes of thought and action, not every regression is pathological and not every regression is permanent. In revolutionary situations, for example, it may be impossible to maintain a coherent sense of self which has continuity, which remains self to self and others, unless one defers, at least temporarily, to a leader. Revolutionary change, in particular, leads to cathectic instability and to the intensification of drives. This establishes the possibility for a search for primary objects, for the consolations and safety of the past. But what revolutionary leaders like Lenin or Robespierre do, or try to do, is force an end to cathectic instability, bring the drives under control, and avoid the regressive pull of primary object relationships. The continued availability of a leader may represent an indispensable prerequisite for the maintenance of coherent ego functions.[36]

We can perhaps best sum up what is meant by our remarks on these last two points with the following example. "That the Romans did not intro-

[35] For an extended discussion of the problem, see Helen B. Lewis, *Shame and Guilt in Neurosis* (New York, 1971), pp. 11–61. Lewis points out that usually shame and guilt are distinguished in developmental or maturational terms—that is, that guilt refers to a higher level of psychic organization than shame. She makes the important assumption "that shame and guilt are equally advanced although different superego functions, developed along different routes of identification." *Ibid.*, p. 23. See also p. 18, for an indication of the great discrepancy in the psychoanalytic literature between discussions of guilt and those of shame. The two quotes on identification from Freud may be found in Parens and Saul, *Dependence in Man*, pp. 44, 50.

[36] It has been observed that "some flow of more or less familiar perceptual stimuli readily capable of integration into one's past experience is necessary for the maintenance of adequate self-observation and evaluation." This is but one psychic process which is interrupted in the course of revolutionary change, necessitating the advent of powerful leaders. Martin H. Stein, "Self-Observation, Reality, and the Superego," in *Psychoanalysis*, ed. Loewenstein *et al.*, p. 277.

duce machines into their economy was by no means due to any kind or form of emotional disorder, but a limitation of the development of the self"; and "what the factor of ego development did was to prevent the realization of what lay within the grasp of Ancient Rome." What is implied in these statements is that a type of socialization process (involving initially the organization of the family) and authority structure (involving subsequently the organization of political, economic, and religious institutions) led to the development of certain ego interests and a certain style of control and mastery over internal and external reality. On the one hand, the analysis is aimed at the level of ego development and object relationships; on the other hand, there is no implication in these statements that the Romans were "neurotic" or "regressive" because their interests took a particular direction or their environment was organized in a particular way.[37]

A fourth error is defining and interpreting behavior as rational or irrational without specifying or being aware of the criteria upon which such a judgment is based. We could have discussed this as another aspect of the third error (the labeling of—especially radical—behavior as regressive). But this is an important point and warrants separate consideration. A glance at the recent spate of psychoanalytic statements on student activism will amply demonstrate that behavior is often dismissed as irrational (as well as unrealistic and immature) on ideological rather than objective grounds.[38] That is, such an evaluation makes sense only if the analyst behaves like the "common sense" man in society and accepts the given social standards as measures of rationality and maturity. However, on the one hand, those standards themselves are open to question on quite legitimate grounds, and, on the other hand, the radical activist has directives, commitments, and value standards of his own.

In this society rational behavior can mean proceeding to action on the basis of evidence, logic, objective analysis, on the basis of choice, judgment, and the calculation of alternatives weighed in the absence of emotion.

---

[37] Kurt R. Eissler, *Medical Orthodoxy and the Future of Psychoanalysis* (New York, 1965), p. 223. The particular quotes raise other questions—the phrasing is such as to imply the evolution of psychic structures. But we do not offer these statements as necessarily accurate interpretations of events; they serve only to establish our point about method.

[38] See, e. g., Robert Michels, "Student Dissent," *J. Amer. Psychoanal. Ass.*, 19, no. 3 (July, 1971): 417–32; and *idem*, "Pseudoanalyzing the Student Rebels," *Psychiatry and the Social Science Review*, 3, no. 5 (1969). Michels is obviously annoyed at other psychoanalysts' treatment of the student question. In part, no doubt, as an object lesson, he turned the analysis around ("Student Dissent," p. 430) as follows: "the well structured symptomatic neurotic is often envious and angry at the apparent freedom of the individual with alloplastic characterologic defenses who responds to conflict by attempting to change the world rather than by adjusting himself to it."

However, it is clear that only under the most special and limited circumstances can anyone begin to approach such an ideal. Scientific endeavor, of course, is organized so that experiments can be repeated, results tested, and conclusions disproved. But even scientific activity is infiltrated by primary processes and ideological considerations. And we could hardly expect the myriad of decisions people make in everyday activity to proceed under such rigorous conditions. We may be committed to rationality as a course of action, but in practice it is hard to control the several criteria by which this is defined.

Rational behavior in this society is also often defined as the treatment of men and objects in instrumental terms, leading to action which, from the standpoint of the actor and societal norms, is the most reasonable in the situation. This definition relies heavily on the agreed upon usefulness of the rational control of affect as a technique. People who behave in these terms may easily assess themselves, and be judged by others, as rational. But such a basis for judging action as rational is hardly rendered according to scientific criteria. Moreover, there are any number of intensely neurotic people who are able to master the aggressive and competitive mandates and not only succeed in terms of what the society deems valuable but, because of that success and mastery, appear to others as "normal." More to the point, rational, conscious processes can themselves be destructive; as D. W. Winnicott put it, "there is much in sanity that is symptomatic."[39]

There is also the problem of nonrational behavior. This refers to any course of action which is directed by value standards which do not themselves oblige rational calculations—for example, religious or aesthetic values. Achievement in these terms cannot be assessed as rational, but it can be assessed as legitimate. Indeed, such behavior may enhance the position of the individual in his group. It may be deemed singular and valuable—as certain ascetic practices often are. It may also be taken as evidence of the willingness of the individual to participate in group activities. Such behavior may then be ego enhancing, providing the actor with a sense of acceptance, worthiness, and accomplishment. In the latter terms, perhaps, most everyday action may therefore be considered nonrational.[40]

---

[39] D. W. Winnicott, *Collected Papers* (London, 1958), p. 150; see also Heinz Hartmann, "On Rational and Irrational Action," *Essays*, p. 65.

[40] The points above are in part adapted from Alfred Schutz, "The Social World and the Theory of Social Action," in *Collected Papers: Studies in Social Theory*, ed. Arvid Brodersen, vol. 2 (The Hague, 1964), pp. 3–19; and Harold Garfinkel, "The Rational Properties of Scientific and Common Sense Activities," *Studies in Ethnomethodology* (Englewood Cliffs, N.J., 1967).

Thus, given the different definitions and qualifications, a lot of activity that is passed off as irrational may easily also be defined as a combination of the rational and the nonrational. This does not mean that there are no criteria for assessing behavior as irrational. On the contrary, we may identify behavior as irrational when, for example, it contradicts and foils the stated goals of the actor, when reality is distorted so that no action taken can ever achieve the ends sought, when judgments are made that could not possibly be correct by objective standards and criteria, and so forth.

One can, therefore, interpret behavior as rational, nonrational, or irrational, conscious or unconscious. But one must proceed cautiously in assigning or implying value to these processes and functions. Even at this point it is still not amiss to note, for example, that unconscious behavior is not necessarily "bad" or that conscious behavior is not necessarily "good." The ego's mechanisms of defense are unconscious, but they are not necessarily pathogenic. The ego functions to avoid anxiety, but also to achieve effective performance, and in pluralized and relatively mobile societies it is just as useful to view the ego and its unconscious functions from the standpoint of a capacity to integrate a variety of complex demands as it is to view the ego as suffering from, or anxious about, what is repressed.

One must proceed cautiously too in assuming that one of these processes or another was operative or dominant in any instance, particularly when dealing with historical actors. In psychoanalytic *therapy*, rational and irrational, conscious and unconscious, processes have been operationalized almost exclusively in terms of the patient's awareness of the symbolic meaning of objects in the contemporary world, or of the awareness of the meaning of fantasies, dreams, images of self and others, or of the intended meanings of action, the realization of possible consequences, and so on. The central issue is *awareness* as the analyst assesses this quality in the light of many meetings between himself and the patient. But the historian does not have his subject as a patient, and, more important, he cannot observe him in relation to the specific objects and circumstances faced and responded to. In fact, all that the historian effectively has—particularly with regard to the study of more remote figures and events—is a highly differentiated theoretical structure which can supplement imagination by describing the widest range of behaviors, and, by analogy with developmental stages, provide the basis for some reasonable judgment as to what emotional commitments to symbolic codes and social objects must have, or could have, meant in a given society at a given time.[41]

The usefulness of psychoanalytic theory cannot be stressed, therefore, without observing also the difficulties involved. The subject is complex and wide open; psychoanalytic theory—to dispel illusions on this score if any are left—is in no sense complete, and it is often lacking precisely in those areas which are of greatest interest to historians and sociologists—for example, character formation. This refers not only to an explanation of how individuals learn to function in terms of the specific demands of a wider society but also to the relationships between and among individuals in terms of social mandates, internalization and identification processes, and those patterns of behavior which are more or less consistent for a population.

Still, these things should be interpreted as a challenge and not as a barrier. One of the interesting aspects of the historian's or the sociologist's work with psychoanalysis is the opportunity presented to reflect on the adequacy of theory and to say something about it, or add to it, in the light of different types of evidence and different vantage points, which are not always or in every respect inferior to the type of evidence that emerges from the clinical situation. In these terms—and from the several standpoints of history, sociology, and psychoanalysis—we have attempted to organize a level and type of analysis not specifically anticipated by psychoanalysis as such.

[41] The historian must also beware of typical or traditional psychoanalytic modes of thought which have been derived from a clinical situation and may not be applicable to historical work. There is, for example, the old cliché, "In the result lies the intention." This expresses the idea that behavior can be explained by its origins in unresolved conflicts, that behavior is unconsciously motivated, and that individuals actively bring on themselves much of what they experience in a passive way. This idea was a necessary corrective to the antiseptic notion that all behavior can be explained in terms of rationality, consciousness, and interest. It is also still useful *in the therapeutic situation*, in that an analyst may want his patient to reflect on something he has done, but for particular, limited, therapeutic reasons. The historian, however, cannot approach a subject on the assumption that, because behavior has an unconscious component, this component is more important than the reality factors in a life situation. Reality is too complex to try and sum it up in these traditional psychoanalytic terms.

Index

THE JOHNS HOPKINS UNIVERSITY PRESS
This book was composed in Baskerville text and
Perpetua display type by the Baltimore Type &
Composition Corp. from a design by James S. Johnston.
It was printed by Universal Lithographers, Inc., on
S. D. Warren's 55-lb. Sebago Antique paper.   The book
was bound by L. H. Jenkins, Inc., in Joanna Ariestox cloth.

Library of Congress Cataloging in Publication Data

Weinstein, Fred, 1931–
    Psychoanalytic sociology.

    Includes bibliographical references.
    1. Sociology—Methodology.   2. Social change.
3. Psychoanalysis—History.   I. Platt, Gerald M.,
joint author.   II. Title.   [DNLM: 1. Psychoanalytic
interpretation.   2. Psychoanalytic theory.   3. Social
change.   WM 460 W424p   1973]
HM26.W44   301'.01'8   72-12860
ISBN 0-8018-1462-6
ISBN 0-8018-1463-4 (pbk)